EDUCATION LIBRARY SERVICE

Browning Way
Woodford Park Industrial Estate
Winsford
CW7 2JN

KT-405-466

Sophie Conran's
SOUPS AND STEWS

For Elkin,
for making the sun
shine every day

Sophie Conran's

SOUPS AND STEWS

CHESHIRE
LIBRARIES

1 9 JAN 2010

RL

Collins

CONTENTS

6   *Introduction*

10   BEEF SOUP AND STEWS

44   LAMB SOUPS AND STEWS

62   PORK SOUPS AND STEWS

80   GAME SOUPS AND STEWS

100   CHICKEN SOUPS AND STEWS

122   FISH SOUPS AND STEWS

148   VEGETABLE SOUPS AND STEWS

180   USEFUL EXTRAS

190   *Index*

192   *Acknowledgements*

Introduction

Beautiful Soup, so rich and green
Waiting in a hot tureen!
Who for such dainties would not stoop?
Soup of the evening, beautiful soup!
Beautiful Soup!
Who cares for fish
Game, or any other dish?
Who would not give all else for two
Pennyworth only of beautiful soup

Lewis Carroll *Alice in Wonderland*

Soups and stews are nourishing, nurturing, satisfying and comforting. From light and delicate to filling and warming, there's a soup or stew for every mood and occasion. A steaming pot is a delight to behold and once placed in front of you, can dissolve all the worries of the world.

The story of soups and stews is as ancient as that of cooking itself and goes back to the dawn of culinary time. Throughout the centuries, and across many cultures, soups and stews have played an important part in the world's culinary history. Over 8,000 years ago, the first primitive tribes would boil foods together to make a sort of stew, and tribes in the Amazonian jungles used turtle shells in which to cook their meat. As for written records, some of the oldest cookbooks dating back to Roman times, contain recipes for lamb and fish stews. There is even a mention of stews in the world's most popular book of all time, the Bible. In the Book of Genesis, Esau offers a meal of lentil stew to his brother Jakob in return for his inheritance. He must have been very hungry!

There is a fine line distinguishing stew from soup. The ingredients of a stew may be chunkier than those of a soup and retain more of their individual flavours; a stew may have thicker liquid and is more likely to be eaten as a main course. While a stew can be cooked on either the hob or in the oven, soups are almost always cooked on the hob. The choice of name is largely a matter of custom; it is often possible for the same dish to be described as soup or stew – in fact the only thing a soup can be, that a stew is definitely not, is smooth. Soups and stews take a while to cook and are best simmered very slowly, so be patient. They are wonderfully humble and inexpensive to make, mostly using the cheaper cuts of meat.

These cuts are best enjoyed once they have been cooked for hours; cook them too fast and all the flavours escape, leaving the meat dry and tasteless. You must make sure the pot never boils, but ever so slightly quivers with the occasional 'plop plop' of rising bubbles. I like to use organic meat, and since these dishes often require the less expensive cuts, they are within the reach of the average household budget. The beautiful thing about soups and stews is that they can nearly always be stretched a little bit further, so are accommodating if an extra guest turns up out of the blue. Plus they improve with age, as the flavours mature and become more fabulous. A three- day-old stew is a rare thing (having usually been gobbled up in minutes), but a truly delicious one.

My wonderful and inspirational mother cooked many of these warming and nourishing dishes for our family from recipes she excavated from ancient crumbling manuscripts. Ever the explorer, she resurrected magnificent dishes from an era that had never heard of convenience food nor was obsessed with fads and fashions, but was bound by the seasons, accepting no less than exceptional quality. It is these amazing meals that have become the bedrock of my own culinary landscape and adventures. Within these pages you will also find recipes from some of my closest friends and family – cooks, chefs and food-writers of immense accomplishment – and I am extremely proud to be able to include them in this collection.

The recipes in this book come from around the world, with many well-known favourites, as well as other little gems that I have adapted to be easily made at home. You'll also find some much-loved British classics – the soups and stews of my childhood, which remain my true loves. All have been tried and tested on my hungry family and friends over the years. I use weights and measurements as a guide, but each recipe is simply my own version, so feel free to adapt, add and omit ingredients at will. Some of these recipes are as ancient as the hills and have grown and changed as they have passed through the kitchens of generation after generation of loving cooks. It seems only right that they continue to stay alive.

I hope you will enjoy making these recipes yourself, the wonderful smells, the anticipation of the loveliness to come and, finally, the joy of eating them with those who you love and cherish. Good health and happy days.

BEEF SOUPS

BEEF AND BARLEY SOUP

HEARTY BEEF SOUP

OXTAIL SOUP

BROWN WINDSOR SOUP

BURGUNDY BEEF WITH MUSHROOMS

ARTICHOKE AND LEMON SOUP

SHABU-SHABU

PASTA IN BRODO

BEEF STEWS

MR PIANIM'S BEEF CURRY

BEEF, BEER AND MUSHROOM STEW WITH CHEESY DUMPLINGS

BOEUF BOURGUIGNON

BOEUF EN DAUBE

Jeremy Lee's
FEATHERBLADE

BOLLITO MISTO

Tom Conran's
CRAZY HOMIES EXTERMINATOR CHILLI

CARBONNADE À LA FLAMANDE

OSSO BUCCO AND RISOTTO MILANESE

Beef

BEEF AND BARLEY SOUP

I am immensely fond of barley. I find it a soothing and comforting ingredient as it has a soft nuttiness that makes this soup ideal for calming frayed nerves.

TO SERVE FOUR TO SIX

1 tbsp olive oil
100g/3½oz bacon lardons
2 braising steaks *about 300g/11oz each*
1 large carrot *peeled and diced*
4 shallots *peeled and diced*
1 rib of celery *cleaned, trimmed and finely chopped*

150ml/5fl oz red wine
8 juniper berries *crushed*
2 large handfuls of pearl barley
½ tbsp tomato purée
1 handful of chopped fresh flat-leaf parsley
sea salt and freshly ground black pepper

Heat the oil in a large pot. Add the lardons and cook until browned. Season the steaks with salt and pepper; add them to the pot and cook until browned on each side, then remove and set aside. Turn down the heat. Gently fry the vegetables with the bacon for about 5 minutes.

Return the steaks to the pot and lay them on top of the vegetables then pour over the wine. Sprinkle in the juniper berries and pearl barley, then stir in the tomato purée and cover with water. Leave to gently simmer for 2 hours, topping up with hot water if it looks like it is drying out.

Remove the steaks from the soup and stir in the parsley. Season to taste. Trim the fat from the steaks and chuck it in the bin. Slice the steaks into 1cm/½ inch strips and divide between the bowls. Ladle in the soup and serve with warm rolls and butter.

HEARTY BEEF SOUP

This is a real crowd pleaser and filling to boot. One of the most satisfying soups I know.

TO SERVE SIX

1 tbsp olive oil
100g/3½oz pancetta *cut into 1cm/½ inch cubes*
300g/11oz chuck steak *cut into 1cm/½ inch sticks*
2 tbsp plain flour *seasoned with salt and pepper*
1 handful of dried porcini mushrooms (ceps) *soaked in boiling water for 20 minutes*
1 onion *peeled and chopped*
2 red peppers *cored, seeded and cut into 1cm/½ inch strips*

2 ribs of celery *cleaned, trimmed and chopped*
3 cloves of garlic *peeled and chopped*
1 tsp finely chopped fresh thyme leaves
½ tsp harissa
300ml/10fl oz tomato passata
600ml/1 pint water
2 handfuls of Puy lentils
sea salt

Heat the oil in a large pan with a lid. Drop in the pancetta and fry until it browns and the fat starts to run out. Remove from the pan and set aside. Meanwhile, dust the beef cubes with the flour and add them to the pan. Fry on all sides until browned, then remove from the pan and set aside with the pancetta.

Chop the porcini, reserving the soaking liquid as it is very flavourful, and add to the pan with the onion, red peppers and celery. Fry the vegetables gently until they are all soft – about 45 minutes. Keep an eye on them and give them a stir every now and again. Once the vegetables are really luscious, stir in the garlic, thyme and harissa and cook through for another couple of minutes.

Stir in the meat and the liquid from the mushrooms and, using a wooden spoon, scrape up anything that is stuck to the bottom of the pan into a sauce. Pour in the passata, water and lentils, stir through and season with a little salt. Bring to a gentle boil, cover with the lid and simmer for 2 hours, stirring every now and then. Add a little water if it starts to become dry.

Season to taste and serve with warm crusty rolls and plenty of butter.

OXTAIL SOUP

This hearty soup brings back lovely warm childhood memories for me. Even when served at school, it was a more than palatable dish that would make an afternoon on the achingly cold, muddy playing field, being whacked by a lacrosse stick, more bearable. This is best made the day before so that you can scoop off the surface fat.

TO SERVE FOUR TO SIX

2 whole oxtails *jointed and trimmed of fat (ask your butcher to do this)*
plain flour *seasoned with salt and pepper*
2 tbsp olive oil
4 carrots *peeled and trimmed*
4 baby turnips *peeled and trimmed (optional)*
8 shallots *peeled and trimmed*
1 leek *cleaned and trimmed*

2 ribs of celery *cleaned and trimmed*
100g/3½oz butter
1 bay leaf
1 small bunch of fresh flat-leaf parsley
½ tbsp Worcestershire sauce
½ tbsp tomato purée
1 tsp ground allspice
sea salt and freshly ground black pepper

Toss the oxtail in the seasoned flour. Heat the oil in a large saucepan, add the oxtail and brown on all sides. Put half of the veg and the butter into the pan with the bay leaf and parsley. Cut the rest of the veg into cubes and keep aside for later. Fill the pan with water and stir in the Worcestershire sauce, tomato purée and allspice. Allow to gently simmer for 2 hours.

Remove the vegetables and bay leaf from the pan and discard. Pop the reserved chopped vegetables into the pan, lightly season with salt and cook for a further 1½ hours. Add more water if necessary to keep the pieces of meat covered with liquid and stir every now and then, making sure it has not burnt or stuck to the bottom of the pan.

Take the pan from the heat and remove the oxtail pieces from the soup and set aside to cool. Place the soup in the fridge until the fat on top has solidified so you can scoop it off and bin it. While still a little warm, separate the oxtail meat from the bones and wobbly bits, and discard the latter. Once the fat has been removed from the soup, whiz the soup in a blender to a purée. Return the meat to the soup and heat through. Season to taste. Serve with warm seeded rolls. It's also great with a blob of horseradish sauce on top.

BROWN WINDSOR SOUP

This is a delicious soup dearly loved by the Victorians and Edwardians. Occasionally, cooked basmati rice is added to Classic Brown Windsor just before serving.

TO SERVE SIX

1 tbsp beef dripping or olive oil
500g/1lb 2oz veal shins *sliced 3mm/ ⅛ inch thick*
1 pinch of ground nutmeg
knob of butter
1 large carrot *peeled and chopped*
1 Spanish onion *sliced*
2 leeks, white part only *chopped*
1 tsp finely chopped fresh thyme leaves

1 bunch of parsley *chopped*
1.5 litres/2½ pints home made beef stock or consommé
1 bay leaf
½ tsp cayenne pepper
1 small glass of sherry or Madeira
sea salt and freshly ground pepper

Heat the dripping or oil in a large pan with a lid over a medium/high heat. Season the veal with a little salt, nutmeg and pepper, then fry for 3 minutes on each side. Remove the steaks and place on a plate until needed. Reduce the heat and drop the butter, carrot, onion, leeks and thyme into the pan. Gently fry the vegetables, stirring from time to time for about 10–15 minutes or until soft.

Return the meat to the pot, then stir in the parsley, the stock, the bay leaf, the cayenne pepper and a pinch of salt. Cover with the lid and leave to very gently bubble away for 2 hours, making sure it never boils. Remove the bay leaf and set the meat aside on a plate.

Scoop the bone marrow out of the middle of the bones and drop it into the soup (it is not necessary to add the marrow if you don't fancy it, but it does give a wonderful richness to the soup). Allow the soup to cool before blitzing it in a food processor until smooth. Using your hands, break the meat up into small pieces, discarding the bones and any globby bits. Plop the meat into the soup, heat through and stir in the Madeira or sherry just before serving. Serve with white toast and butter.

BURGUNDY BEEF WITH WILD MUSHROOMS

This French recipe brings together some of my most treasured ingredients. Lovely, hefty red wine, gorgeous earthy wild mushrooms and good country smokey bacon. They all combine perfectly to make this superb soup.

TO SERVE SIX

3 tbsp olive oil
100g/3½oz bacon lardons *cut into 1cm/½ inch sticks*
500ml/18fl oz beef stock *(see page 184)*
300g/11oz shallots or pickling onions *peeled*
400g/14oz fresh chanterelle mushrooms
2 cloves of garlic *peeled and chopped*
1 handful of chopped fresh flat-leaf parsley

2 tbsp plain flour
400g/14oz chuck steak *cut into 1cm/½ inch cubes*
4 tbsp marc de Bourgogne or Cognac
½ bottle of red wine *such as Burgundy or something hefty*
sea salt and freshly ground black pepper

Heat 1 tbsp of the oil in a large pan and fry the bacon until it begins to crisp and brown. Pour the stock into a small saucepan and plop in the onions. Simmer gently for 10 minutes. Lift the bacon out of the pan and set aside. Drain the onions, reserving the stock, and fry them with the mushrooms in the bacon fat until beginning to brown. Add the garlic and parsley and stir through, then cook for a couple of minutes, remove from the pan and set aside.

Mix the flour and meat in a bowl and season with salt and pepper. Add the rest of the oil to the pan and fry the meat on all sides until browned. Remove with a slotted spoon and return to the bowl. Pour the marc or Cognac into the pot and bubble, stirring with a wooden spoon to scrape up the flour that has cooked onto the bottom of the pan. Add a little of the wine if it boils dry. Keep stirring until all the flour has been incorporated into the liquid and you have a smooth sauce before adding any more wine.

Return the meat to the pan with the rest of the wine and the reserved stock and stir through. Leave to simmer gently for 2 hours. Stir every now and then and add a little hot water if it starts to get dry. Drop in the bacon, mushrooms and onions, heat through, and add hot water until it reaches your desired consistency. Season to taste and serve with slabs of country bread and fresh butter.

JERUSALEM ARTICHOKE AND LEMON SOUP

I find it quite remarkable that these nuggets of gnarly muddiness can result in something so sublime and luxurious as this beautiful dish. It's like a sophisticated potato soup.

TO SERVE SIX

½ lemon
750g/1lb 11oz Jerusalem artichokes
3 tbsp beef dripping or 2 tbsp olive oil or butter
4 large carrots *peeled and chopped*
2 leeks white parts only *cleaned, trimmed and chopped*

1 parsnip *peeled and chopped*
500ml/18fl oz beef stock *(see page 184)*
2 handfuls of chopped fresh mint
zest of 2 lemons *finely chopped*
salt

Fill a bowl with cold water and squeeze the juice from the lemon into it. Peel and chop the artichokes and put into the acidulated water as you prepare them – this prevents them from going brown.

Heat the dripping, oil or butter in a large pan and gently fry all the vegetables for 20 minutes, stirring every now and again.

Add the stock and 1.5 litres/2½ pints of water to the vegetables, bring to the boil, lower the heat and simmer for 30–40 minutes or until the vegetables are easily squashed with the back of a wooden spoon. Remove from the heat and pour about 500ml/18fl oz of cold water into the pan – this cools it all down so that it is not hot when you purée it.

Whiz the mixture in a blender until smooth. Pour back into the pan reheat and stir through the mint and lemon zest. Season to taste with salt.

SHABU-SHABU

Shabu-Shabu, meaning 'swish swish', is a wonderfully light Japanese hotpot, a little like a fondue. You cook the sliced meat yourself at the table and enjoy the vegetables and stock afterwards. Everyone needs chopsticks or a fork, a spoon and bowl and dipping sauce.

TO SERVE FOUR TO SIX

600g/1lb 5oz beef fillet *sliced as finely as possible and cut into 2cm/¾ inch strips*
1 litre/1¾ pints beef or chicken stock *(see pages 184 and 185)*
2 tbsp soy sauce
2 carrots *peeled and finely sliced*
10 shiitake mushrooms *sliced*
1 bunch of enoki mushrooms *roots cut off*
6 spring onions *trimmed and cut in half lengthways*
1 cube of firm tofu *cut into four pieces (make sure that the tofu is not too fine, something more solid is best)*

75g/3oz udon noodles
2 pak choi *cleaned and sliced*
½ Chinese cabbage *cut into strips*

For the dipping sauce
1 walnut-sized piece of fresh root ginger *peeled and finely chopped*
3 tbsp soy sauce
2 tbsp lime juice
2 tbsp sesame oil

Set the table first with a small paraffin stove or burner that will keep your pot bubbling, the chopsticks, bowls and some napkins. Prepare all the ingredients, arrange the beef slices on a plate, and have them waiting for the arrival of your guests. Combine all the ingredients for the dipping sauce in a bowl and place on the table.

Once your guests are seated, pour the stock, soy sauce and 500ml/18fl oz of water into a large pot (it needs to fit safely on the paraffin stove and be big enough to take all the ingredients). Bring to the boil and then add, in this order, the carrots, mushrooms and spring onions. Then add the noodles, tofu, pak choi and lastly the cabbage.

Carry it very carefully to the table and set on the stove. Now the fun starts – each person should dip their meat into the soup until done to their taste, then dip it into the sauce and devour. Everyone helps themselves to veg, tofu and noodles and lastly the broth, which by this point is superb with wonderful flavours from both the veg and the meat.

PASTA IN BRODO

I adore this dish – it is the Italian equivalent of chicken noodle soup and soothes away life's stresses and strains. I formed my attachment to this soup at the tender age of 11, when my parents took a gastronomic tour of Italy. We whizzed around hairpin bends from Milan to Rome, eating on terraces overlooking fields of wild flowers, and in piazzas with gurgling fountains. Unfortunately, the speedy driving and rich meals took their toll. So I discovered the soothing qualities of pasta in broth and, to my poor father's dismay, ate it for lunch and dinner for the rest of the trip, adoring every mouthful with its little parcels of loveliness.

TO SERVE FOUR TO SIX

1.5 litres/2½ pints excellent beef stock *(see page 184) made with the addition of 3 chicken drumsticks and a small piece of Parmesan rind (odd, but traditional)*

250g/9oz tortellini
freshly grated Parmesan *(optional)*
sea salt and freshly ground black pepper

Reduce the stock by about one-third and season until it is nectar. Refrigerate the stock overnight. By the next day it will have set like jelly and the fat will have formed a crust on the top. This is beef dripping and can be used for frying, or binned if you don't like the look of it and it makes you a bit queasy.

Ladle 1 litre/1¾ pints of stock into a pan and bring to the boil, taste and season with salt. Drop in the tortellini and cook for the time stated on the packet. Serve with the Parmesan sprinkled on top if you wish.

MR PIANIM'S BEEF CURRY

Curry is a big part of the British culinary psyche and I have not been immune. I love grinding my own spices – there seems to be something very satisfying on a primitive level about pounding a few sticks and seeds together to produce some wonderful aromatic flavouring.

TO SERVE FOUR

2 tbsp olive oil
600g/1lb 5oz chuck steak *trimmed and cut into 3cm/1¼ inch cubes*
50g/2oz butter
1 large Spanish onion *peeled and sliced*
1 walnut-sized piece of fresh root ginger *peeled and chopped*
300ml/10fl oz tomato passata
500ml–1 litre/18fl oz–1¾ pints beef or chicken stock *(see pages 184 and 185) or water*
sea salt and freshly ground black pepper

For the curry paste
1 medium-hot dried smoked chilli
3 cardamom pods *crushed and with husks removed*
1 heaped tsp coriander seeds
½ tsp each ground turmeric and cumin
1 pinch of sea salt
3 cloves of garlic *peeled and roughly chopped*
1 pinch of dried curry leaves
a few grinds of black pepper

Grind all the ingredients for the curry paste together in a pestle and mortar or spice grinder. Heat the oil in a large pan over a high heat. Season the steak with salt and pepper, drop into the pan and cook until browned on all sides. Remove with a slotted spoon and keep aside. Reduce the heat, drop the butter into the pan and gently fry the onion and ginger together until the onion is soft. Stir in the curry paste and fry for about 10 minutes, giving it a gentle poke and stir around from time to time.

Glug in the passata and 500ml/18fl oz of stock or water. Return the meat to the pan, stir through and leave to gently simmer for 2 hours. Check that it isn't burning or sticking from time to time and add a little more stock or water if it looks like it is drying out.

I like to serve this curry with basmati rice cooked in stock and tossed with butter, and a dish of spinach that has been briefly boiled then tossed in a pan with cream and a little nutmeg.

BEEF, BEER AND MUSHROOM STEW WITH CHEESY DUMPLINGS

My lovely mum is a fabulous cookery writer and as kids we were her happy guinea pigs. A couple of her books were on British cooking and I have the fondest memories of dumplings with lots of gravy. My version has the addition of baking powder to make them very light and fluffy; if you prefer a more solid dumpling, you can omit it from the recipe.

TO SERVE SIX

600g/1lb 5oz stewing steak *cubed*
2 tbsp plain flour *seasoned with salt and pepper*
2 tbsp olive oil or beef dripping
50g/2oz butter
1 red onion *peeled and chopped*
2 ribs of celery *cleaned, trimmed and chopped*
2 carrots *peeled and chopped*
350g/12oz brown mushrooms *trimmed, quartered*
2 leeks *cleaned, trimmed and chopped*
1 tsp paprika

500ml/18fl oz light beer or lager
freshly ground black pepper

For the dumplings
100g/4oz self-raising flour
50g/2oz prepared suet
¼ tsp baking powder
1 tsp mustard powder
75g/3oz strong grated Cheddar cheese
1 handful of chopped fresh flat-leaf parsley
1 egg *beaten*

Preheat the oven to 180°C/350°F/gas mark 4. Roll the meat in the seasoned flour until coated. Heat the oil or dripping in a large pot with a lid and brown the meat in two batches. Pop the meat in a bowl until needed. Reduce the heat and plop the butter into the pot, throw in all the vegetables, the paprika and a good grind of black pepper and give it a proper stir. Gently fry for about 25 minutes until soft, keeping an eye on them and stirring every few minutes, as you don't want them to burn. Return the meat to the pot. Glug in the beer or lager and enough water to just cover the meat, stir through, pop the lid on the pot and place in the oven for 1¾ hours.

Meanwhile, make the dumplings. Mix all the dry ingredients together in a large bowl. Using a fork, briskly mix in the egg and enough water to make a sticky dough but do not over-mix. Form into dumplings the size of walnuts and pop on top of the stew at the end of the cooking time, cover the pot and cook for a further 15 minutes. Serve with a salad on the side if you like, but it is a whole meal on its own.

BOEUF BOURGUIGNON

Jane Grigson called boeuf à la bourguignon (beef in the Burgundy style), 'The stew of stews.' This rich, delicious dish is worthy of a good-quality red wine.

TO SERVE SIX

1.5kg/3lb 15oz chuck stewing or braising steak *cut into 4cm/1½ inch cubes*
30g/1¼oz plain flour *seasoned with salt and pepper*
4 tbsp olive oil
125g/4oz pancetta *cut into little sticks*
½ bottle of full-bodied red wine *such as Merlot or Burgundy*

300ml/10fl oz beef stock *(see page 184)*
1 bouquet garni
20 pearl (or 'button') onions *peeled and trimmed*
225g/8oz button mushrooms
25g/1oz butter
sea salt and freshly ground black pepper

Preheat the oven to 150°C/300°F/gas mark 2. Coat the beef cubes thoroughly with the seasoned flour. Heat half the oil in a large ovenproof pan with a lid on a high heat. Fry the pancetta in the oil until browned, then remove it from the pan. Add the meat and fry, adding a little more oil if necessary. Fry the meat in batches, putting in just as many pieces as will cover the bottom of the pan, until browned. Set the meat aside with the pancetta.

Reduce the heat to medium to low, pour in half the wine and bring to the boil, using a wooden spoon to scrape up the gubbins that have stuck to the bottom. Return the meat and pancetta to the pan. Pour in the rest of the wine and just enough of the stock to leave the top halves of the uppermost pieces of meat showing above the liquid. Add the bouquet garni, stir and season with pepper. Pop the lid on the pan and simmer in the oven for 2 hours. Meanwhile, simmer the onions in a small pan in the remaining stock for 5 minutes. Remove the onions and discard the stock. Fry the onions and mushrooms gently in the rest of the oil and the butter for 10 minutes, and then set aside until needed.

Once the meat has finished simmering, remove the bouquet garni and stir the onions and mushrooms through. Taste for seasoning. I like to serve with mashed potatoes (see page 187) and buttered Savoy cabbage.

BOEUF EN DAUBE

This is a classic stew from Provence, made using either white or red wine. Daube is traditionally served with noodles and often made with the meat of bulls killed in bullfights, which still take place in the region. It's named after 'dobar', the Spanish word for stew.

TO SERVE FOUR TO SIX

1kg/2¼lb chuck steak *cut into 5cm/2 inch cubes*
2 tbsp olive oil
150g/5oz pancetta *cut into small cubes*
1 red pepper *cored, seeded and sliced*
2 red onions *peeled and chopped*
100g/3½oz black olives
150ml/5fl oz beef stock *(see page 184)*
400g tin of chopped plum tomatoes
2 anchovies *chopped*
2 strips of orange zest *(use a potato peeler)*

1 handful of rinsed capers *(optional)*
salt and freshly ground black pepper

For the marinade
150ml/5fl oz white wine
1 tbsp olive oil
3 cloves of garlic *peeled, bashed and cut in half*
1 tsp each finely chopped fresh
thyme and rosemary
freshly ground black pepper

Combine all the ingredients for the marinade in a bowl, add the beef and stir through. Leave to stand for a couple of hours or overnight, stirring occasionally. When ready to cook, preheat the oven to 150°C/300°F/gas mark 2. Heat half the oil in a large pan with a lid, pop the pancetta into the pan and cook, stirring, until it begins to brown. Stir in the red pepper, onions and olives and fry for 10 minutes.

Heat the remaining oil in another pan until smoking. Drain the beef from the marinade (reserving the marinade) and fry the beef in batches for 3 minutes on each side until brown. Add to the pan with the onion mixture, and deglaze the pan the beef was fried in with the stock. Pour the stock over the meat, stir in the tomatoes, reserved marinade, anchovies and orange zest , stir through and pop into the oven for 2 hours. Check after 1 hour and top up with water if it starts to dry out. Once it is cooked through, stir in the capers, if using, taste and adjust the seasoning. Add a little boiling water if it is a bit dry. Serve with plain boiled potatoes tossed in butter and parsley, a tomato salad and a big green salad. It is also lovely with couscous.

Jeremy Lee's
FEATHERBLADE

Jeremy is a fantastic chef and his wit is sharper than any knife and keener than the strongest mustard. His smile and cooking can brighten any day. In this recipe, the featherblade, a piece of shoulder of beef, is cooked very slowly on the gentlest of heats until tender.

TO SERVE TEN TO TWELVE MOST HEARTILY

6 tbsp olive oil
1 piece of featherblade of beef *about 2.5kg/5½lb*
150g/5oz unsalted butter
6 fresh sage leaves
1 generous sprig each of fresh thyme and rosemary
10 cloves of garlic *unpeeled*
250g/9oz lentils *those from Puy are excellent*
1 small onion *peeled and finely chopped*
1 small carrot *peeled and finely chopped*
1 rib of celery *peeled and finely chopped*

2 cloves garlic *peeled and finely chopped*
1 bay leaf

For the green sauce
tight fistful of picked fresh flat-leaf parsley
4 anchovy fillets *coarsely chopped*
1 tsp of capers *coarsely chopped*
2 cloves of garlic *peeled and finely chopped*
2 tbsp olive oil
1 tbsp very good red wine vinegar
sea salt and plenty of freshly ground black pepper

Place a heavy-bottomed pot on a gentle heat and pour in 2 tablespoons of the oil. Liberally salt and pepper the featherblade, ensuring a thoroughly even seasoning rubbed all over. Place the meat in the heated oil and let it sit until darkened and well coloured, without singeing. Move and repeat until the whole piece is marvellously crusted all over.

Remove the joint, discard any oil and wipe the pan, leaving only the gunk adhering to the bottom and sides of the pan. Add in the butter and 2 tablespoons of fresh oil. Throw in the herbs and then return the beef, rolling altogether. Add a cup or so of water and stand back, then reduce the heat to a little murmur and place a lid upon the pot. Let the joint cook quietly for 4–6 hours until the piece is soft and tender. Roll the joint occasionally to prevent sticking and add a little water every now and then to keep the whole thing merry.

While the beef continues on its way, attention now turns towards the lentils. Tip the lentils into a sieve and rinse very well under cold, running water. Put the lentils into a pot, cover with cold water and set this upon a high heat and bring to a boil. Tip the lentils into a colander and rinse lightly under cold water. Pour the remaining oil into a pan then add the carrot, onion, celery and garlic.Fry gently for ten minutes or so, stirring frequently, then add the lentils and the bay leaf and enough water to cover. Bring to a simmer and leave to cook, a lid upon the pot, for a few hours until very tender.

Once the pots are simmering, make the green sauce. Wash the leaves very well, leave them to dry, then place in a bowl with the anchovies, capers and garlic. Pour in the oil and the vinegar stirring together very well.

Remove the beef to a splendid dish. Add some water to the pot, up the heat and stir well lifting up any scraps adhering to the bottom of the pot. Tip the warm lentils into this, then add the green sauce. Pour this over the beef and take triumphantly to the table where folks can help themselves.

BOLLITO MISTO

Bollito misto, as its name suggests, is mixed boiled meat. It is the Italian equivalent of boiled beef and carrots, totally delicious and almost as easy to make as a boiled egg. The list of meat is only a guide – add or omit meats as you like.

TO SERVE EIGHT TO TEN

1 small veal tongue *about 1kg/2¼lb, trimmed of all bones (I like to tie mine with string in a roll)*
1 ham hock *about 1kg/2¼lb*
2 onions *peeled*
4 carrots *peeled*

½ celeriac *peeled and cubed*
1 small chicken
1 bay leaf
1 Cotechino *(pork boiling sausage)*

Fill a very large pot three-quarters full with water and bring to the boil. Drop in the tongue and ham and simmer for 1½ hours.

Plop the veg, chicken and bay leaf into the pot and continue simmering for another 30 minutes. Take the tongue out and leave to cool, then peel the skin off the tongue and chuck the skin away. Cook the Cotechino as directed on the package. Return the tongue to the pot and continue cooking for another 30 minutes.

Serve all the meat cut in slices, with plain boiled potatoes tossed in butter and parsley, some lentils and a few sauces. My favourite is salsa verde, but a home-made mayonnaise with a little grated fresh horseradish is delicious, as is *mostarda di cremona* and Dijon mustard. Serve with or without the broth and boiled vegetables.

Tom Conran's
CRAZY HOMIES
EXTERMINATOR CHILLI

Tom, my exceptional brother, owns a fantastic Mexican restaurant in London, Crazy Homies. We recommend drinking margueritas with this chilli for a real party.

TO SERVE TEN TO TWELVE

4 tbsp vegetable oil
2kg/4¼lb minced beef
2 large onions *peeled and finely chopped*
3 fresh jalapeno chillies *finely chopped*
3 tbsp crushed cumin seeds
2 tbsp dried oregano
2 tbsp ground coriander
1 tbsp ground cinnamon
1 tbsp chilli powder
1 tbsp paprika
375ml/13fl oz beer

500ml/18fl oz beef stock *(see page 184)*
875g/1lb 15oz crushed tomatoes
1kg/2¼lb cooked kidney or pinto beans
sea salt and freshly ground black pepper

For the garnish
soured cream
grated sharp Cheddar cheese
chopped spring onions
salsa

Warm 1 tablespoon of the oil in a large pan over a medium heat and brown the beef all over. Set aside. Add the rest of the oil to the pan and sweat the onions gradually until they start to colour brown (this stage is very important and gives the dish a lot of flavour).

Add the chopped chillies and sauté a minute longer, then add the herbs and spices and cook for a further 2 minutes. Add the beef, beer, beef stock and tomatoes, bring up to the boil and then simmer, partially covered, for 1 hour, stirring occasionally. Stir in the beans and cook for another 30 minutes. Season with salt and pepper.

This probably tastes better the next day when the flavours have had a chance to meld. Garnish with the sour cream, cheese, onions and salsa.

TIP You can play with the spicing to your own tastes – add allspice, fennel seed, other chillies, orange zest, and so on. Go to www.lucky7london.co.uk for an update on Tom's restaurants.

CARBONNADE À LA FLAMANDE

This is a traditional Belgian dish dating back to the 14th century. I am afraid I have doctored it slightly by using a light beer instead of dark, but the result is fabulous.

TO SERVE TWO

2 tbsp olive oil
700g/4½lb chuck steak *cut into two large steaks*
1 tbsp butter
4 red onions *peeled and finely sliced*
1 tbsp red wine vinegar
1 tbsp dark brown sugar

400ml/14fl oz light Belgian beer
1 bouquet garni
1 tbsp Dijon mustard
2 tbsp Worcestershire sauce
3 tbsp double cream
sea salt and freshly ground black pepper

Preheat the oven to 180°C/350°F/gas mark 4. Heat the oil in a large pan with a lid on a very high heat until smoking. Season the steaks with salt and pepper and fry without turning for about 3 minutes on each side or until they have a brown crust. Remove the steaks to a plate and reduce the heat. Drop the butter into the pan and stir in the onions. Cook, stirring every now and then, for about 10 minutes until they are soft. Pour in the vinegar and sugar and give the onions a good stir. Continue stirring every now and again for another 10 minutes or until the onions have become caramelised and slightly gooey.

Return the steaks to the pan, pour the beer over them and drop in the bouquet garni. Bring to a gentle simmer, then cover with the lid and pop in the oven for 3 hours, checking every hour or so to make sure it is not drying out. Add some water if it is, to keep it moist, and turn over the pieces of meat. Remove the pan from the oven and put it back on the hob. Transfer the meat to a plate and discard the herbs. Turn up the heat and reduce the sauce to about half the quantity.

Meanwhile, mix the mustard, Worcestershire sauce and cream in a bowl. Once the sauce has reduced, slice the meat into 2cm/¾ inch strips and return to the pan with any juice. Stir in the cream and mustard mixture and heat through. Serve with mashed potatoes (see page 187), and carrots tossed in butter and chopped tarragon.

OSSO BUCCO
AND RISOTTO MILANESE

My son Felix goes nuts for osso bucco which literally means bone with a hole – it is his favourite dish. The meat becomes so tender, you can cut it with a spoon. With or without the gremolata, it is an easy and satisfying stew.

TO SERVE FOUR

2 tbsp olive oil
4 large pieces of veal shin, or osso bucco *with bones in (about 2kg/4¼lb in total)*
1 tbsp plain flour *seasoned with salt and pepper*
50g/2oz butter
1 large red onion *peeled and chopped*
1 rib of celery *cleaned, trimmed and chopped*
2 cloves of garlic *peeled and chopped*
150ml/5fl oz white wine
400g tin of plum tomatoes
about 150ml/5fl oz beef stock *(see page 184)*
2 strips of orange peel *(use a potato peeler)*
sea salt and freshly ground black pepper

For the risotto
2 tbsp olive oil
100g/3½oz butter
1 Spanish onion *peeled and finely chopped*
3 cloves of garlic *peeled and finely chopped*
5 handfuls of risotto rice
(1 for each person and 1 for the pot)
150ml/5fl oz white wine
about 1.5 litres/2½ pints chicken stock *(see page 185)*
1 large pinch of saffron threads
1 handful of freshly grated Parmesan
sea salt to taste

For the gremolata
2 cloves of garlic *peeled and finely chopped*
zest of 1 lemon *finely chopped*
1 handful of finely chopped fresh flat-leaf parsley

Heat the oil in a pan with a lid big enough to take the meat all in one layer. Coat the meat in the seasoned flour and fry over a medium to high heat, turning once until lightly browned on both sides. Remove from the pan and set aside.

Reduce the heat, add the butter and gently fry the onion and celery for 10 minutes until the onion is soft. Add the garlic, pour in the wine and scrape the bottom of the pan with a wooden spoon to dislodge any flour sticking to the bottom, then simmer for 5 minutes.

cont.

cont.

Throw in the tomatoes, stock and strips of orange peel, giving the tomatoes a bit of a mash with your spoon. Return the meat to the pan and submerge it in the sauce. Cover the pan and leave to gently simmer for 2 hours, stirring from time to time, turning the meat and adding some water if it starts to dry out.

After about 90 minutes, start making the risotto. Heat the oil and half the butter in a large pan and gently fry the onion for about 10 minutes or until soft and translucent. Stir in the garlic and rice and fry, stirring continuously, for a couple of minutes. Glug in the wine and let it bubble until it is all but evaporated.

Meanwhile, heat the stock in a pan. Ideally, it should be kept warm for the whole process. Sprinkle the saffron and a pinch of salt into the rice and stir through. From now on it's a pretty repetitive process involving adding about a wine glass full of stock and stirring a lot, until the rice has absorbed almost all the stock, then adding some more and repeating.

This should continue until the rice is almost cooked, but with still a tiny little bite to it. Take off the heat and, using a wooden spoon, gently beat the rest of the butter and the Parmesan into the rice.

When your meat is extremely tender and beginning to fall off the bone, it is ready to plate up. Mix together the ingredients for the gremolata in a bowl, and sprinkle on top of the osso bucco. Serve with the risotto.

LAMB SOUPS

WELSH CAWL

SCOTCH BROTH

LAMB AND NOODLES WITH SEVEN PRECIOUS INGREDIENTS

AUBERGINE, LAMB AND CHICKPEA SOUP

LAMB STEWS

Dave Myers & Si King aka 'The Hairy Bikers'
LANCASHIRE HOTPOT

SPICED LAMB WITH BEANS

LAMB SHANKS WITH CARAMELISED ONION

MEXICAN LAMB

SPANISH LAMB SHOULDER WITH TOMATOES AND OLIVES

Vicki Conran's
IRISH STEW

LAMB WITH PRESERVED LEMON

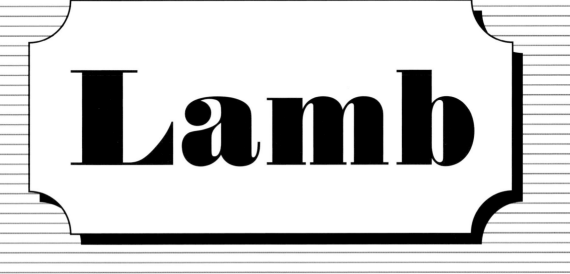

WELSH CAWL

This soup is as Welsh as dragons and has its roots in the mists of time. I am not sure why it is called cawl – I have found some reference to the caul being a sheep's stomach and occasionally being used as one of the ingredients. However, cawl nowadays seems to mean soup in Welsh and there are as many varieties as there are mountains in Wales. It is reputed to taste even better if you gently sing in Welsh as the pot simmers.

TO SERVE SIX TO EIGHT

1kg/2¼lb lamb shoulder *bone in*
1 large onion *peeled and roughly chopped*
7 peppercorns
1 handful of chopped fresh flat-leaf parsley,
plus 1 handful of fresh parsley to serve
50g/2oz butter

1 small swede *peeled and cut into 2cm/¾ inch cubes*
1 large parsnip *peeled and cut into 2cm/¾ inch cubes*
3 carrots *peeled and cut into 2cm/¾ inch cubes*
2 large potatoes *peeled and cut into 2cm/¾ inch cubes*
2 leeks *cleaned, trimmed and finely sliced*
sea salt and freshly ground pepper

Put the lamb, onion, peppercorns and parsley into a large pot and cover with water. Bring to a very gentle boil, then simmer for 2 hours. Skim off any foam or scum that rises to the surface and throw it away. Take off the heat and allow to cool.

Remove the meat to a bowl and strain the stock. Refrigerate the stock until the fat solidifies and can be scraped off (see Tip). Strip the meat from the bones and fat, keeping it in big chunks. Discard the fat and bones. Melt the butter in a large pot and fry all the chopped veg except the leeks for about 10 minutes or until beginning to brown, not forgetting to stir every now and again. Pour the stock and meat into the veg and bring to a gentle simmer for 15 minutes. Transfer the chunks of meat to a bowl to cool, add the leeks to the soup and continue to bubble. When the meat is cool enough to handle, cut off any wobbly bits and discard, then cut the meat into bite-sized pieces. Return to the pot, season to taste and serve with fresh parsley stirred through, a chunk of Cheddar, white rolls and fresh butter.

TIP You can also take off the fat by throwing a handful of ice into the stock to cool it quickly, then scooping out the ice and discarding it – the fat clings to the ice.

SCOTCH BROTH

This is a million miles away from the gloopy, stodgy stuff you get in a can. Try making it with beef instead of lamb or lentils instead of split peas. I am not a fan of turnips so I always use a swede, but you can use either or both if you like.

TO SERVE SIX

3 large carrots *peeled*
600g/1lb 5oz lamb neck or shoulder *bones in*
1 handful of dried split green peas
1 handful of pearl barley
1 bay leaf
1 rib of celery *cleaned and trimmed*
1 onion *peeled and sliced*

2 leeks, *cleaned trimmed and sliced*
1 turnip or swede *peeled and cubed (optional)*
½ Savoy cabbage *trimmed, cored and sliced*
1 pinch of nutmeg
1 handful of chopped fresh flat-leaf parsley
sea salt and freshly ground black pepper

Slice two of the carrots, leave the third whole. Put the meat, dried peas, pearl barley, bay leaf, the whole carrot and the celery into a large pot. Fill with about 2.5 litres/4¼ pints of water and bring to the boil, then gently simmer for 1 hour. Skim off any foam or scum that rises to the surface and throw it away.

After an hour, bin the celery, bay leaf and carrot and then add all the remaining veg except the cabbage to the pot and continue to simmer for a further hour. The cabbage can then be plopped into the simmering pot with the nutmeg and cooked for 20 minutes.

Take the pot off the heat and remove the pieces of meat. Allow them to cool for a while, then strip the meat from the bones and wobbly bits. Drop the meat back into the soup, binning the bones and bits. Season to taste, stir through the parsley and serve with warm crusty rolls and butter.

LAMB AND NOODLES WITH SEVEN PRECIOUS INGREDIENTS

In Chinese cooking the ingredients are revered and that is why this dish is resplendent with its seven precious ingredients – lemon, ginger, star anise, cinnamon, sugar, soy sauce and sherry vinegar. They elevate it to another level of yumminess.

TO SERVE SIX TO EIGHT

2 tbsp olive oil
1.5kg/3lb 5oz shoulder of lamb *bone in*

For the broth
1 walnut-sized piece of fresh root ginger *peeled and quartered*
2 star anise
1 cinnamon stick
1 strip of lemon peel *(cut with a potato peeler)*
1 tbsp soft dark brown sugar
100ml/3½fl oz dark soy sauce
50ml/2fl oz sherry vinegar

For the soup
2 carrots *peeled and finely sliced*
50g/2oz shiitake mushrooms *sliced*
100g/3½oz enoki mushrooms *trimmed*
½ Chinese cabbage
75g/3oz noodles *(fine rice or soba)*
1 large handful of bean sprouts
1 handful of fresh coriander leaves *(optional)*

Heat the oil in a large pan and fry the lamb on both sides briefly until browned. Cover with water, add all the ingredients for the broth and gently simmer for 2 hours. Skim off any foam or scum that rises to the surface and throw it away.

Take the meat out of the pan and strain the broth, discarding the gubbins and removing as much fat as possible. Clean the pan and return the broth to it, keeping the meat aside. Bring the broth to the boil and drop in the carrots. Bubble for a couple of minutes, then add the mushrooms, cabbage, noodles and bean sprouts. Boil for a further 3–5 minutes.

Meanwhile, slice the meat. Serve the soup in bowls with the meat on top and garnished with a few coriander leaves if you like.

AUBERGINE, LAMB AND CHICKPEA SOUP

A really wonderful soup for any time of year. I like to serve it with chunks of sourdough bread, and I sometimes stir in fresh spinach at the end.

TO SERVE SIX TO EIGHT

For the broth
1kg/2¼lb lamb breast *bones in, as meaty as possible*
1 leek *cleaned and trimmed*
1 bunch of fresh mint
3 carrots *peeled*
2 dried chillies
200ml/7fl oz white wine

For the soup
400g tin of chickpeas *drained*
2 tbsp olive oil

50g/2oz butter
2 onions *peeled and chopped*
10cm/4 inch piece of Spanish chorizo *cut into 1cm/½ inch slices*
1 aubergine *trimmed peeled and chopped*
3 cloves of garlic *peeled and chopped*
1 tsp cumin powder
10 tomatoes *peeled, seeded and chopped (see page 121)*
1 large handful each of chopped fresh coriander and mint
sea salt and freshly ground black pepper

Put all the ingredients for the broth in a large pot with a lid. Cover with plenty of water and bring to a gentle boil. Cover with the lid, reduce the heat and leave to bubble slowly for 2 hours. Meanwhile, heat the oil and butter in a large pan, throw in the onions and chorizo and gently fry for 10 minutes. Stir in the aubergine, garlic and cumin, grind in some black pepper and fry for a further 15 minutes. Keep an eye on it and give it a stir – the aubergine sponges up all the butter and oil and it can then burn.

Pour in the tomatoes and season with a good pinch of salt. Keep an eye on the pot and stir every now and then for about 1 hour or until it becomes dark red and the consistency of a thick sauce.

Strain the precious liquid into a bowl, discarding the vegetables and mint, but keep the meat. Remove as much meat as you can and chuck the bones and globby bits in the bin. Stir the meat, chickpeas and broth into the tomato mixture and simmer for a further 10 minutes. Stir through the mint and coriander. Serve with warm pitta bread and olive oil.

Dave Myers & Si King aka 'The Hairy Bikers'
LANCASHIRE HOTPOT

Bumping into Dave and Si at foodie events always makes my day. Their hotpot is the ultimate comforting stew with both kidney and black pudding. It is rich and irresistible.

TO SERVE FOUR TO SIX

50g/2oz butter, cut into cubes *plus extra to grease*
2 tbsp olive oil
1kg/2¼lb neck of lamb *boned and diced*
4 lamb kidneys *cored and trimmed into quarters*
2 onions *peeled and sliced*
1 tbsp plain flour
250ml/9fl oz lamb stock

1 sprig of fresh thyme
2 bay leaves
1kg/2¼lb good old potatoes *peeled and sliced*
2 black pudding rings *skinned and sliced*
1 tsp Worcestershire sauce
sea salt and freshly ground black pepper

Preheat the oven to 180°C/350°F/gas mark 4. Butter a lidded casserole dish.

Warm the oil in a pan, brown the lamb and kidneys, then remove from the pan and set aside. Add the onion and ½ teaspoon of salt to the pan, to draw out the moisture, and sweat for a couple of minutes. Add the flour and coat the onions, then add the stock, thyme and bay leaves. Stir to make a lovely thickened gravy, then discard the herbs.

Place a layer of potatoes on the bottom of the dish and season. Add half the lamb and kidney mixture, then a layer of black pudding slices, about half will do. Pour over half the gravy. Then cover with a layer of potato slices, seasoning the potatoes as you go with Worcestershire sauce and salt and pepper and, as before, a layer of meat, then black pudding, then gravy. The top layer of potatoes can be arranged as carefully as you like to make a nice scalloped pattern or funky circles. Dot with the butter cubes.

Cover with the lid and place in the oven for 20 minutes, then take off the lid and cook for a further 20 minutes until the top layer of spuds is golden. Ecky thump lad, this is champion.

SPICED LAMB WITH BEANS

With its deliciously rich gravy and meltingly tender meat, this is a truly comforting stew, which will fill your belly and put a smile on your face.

TO SERVE SIX

1kg/2¼lb boneless lamb *either leg or shoulder, cut into 4cm/1½ inch chunks*
2 tbsp olive oil
50g/2oz butter
2 red onions *peeled and chopped*
3 garlic cloves *peeled and chopped*
1 tsp paprika

1 tsp ground cumin
1 tsp crushed dried chilli
150ml/5fl oz white wine
400g tin of plum tomatoes
400g tin of borlotti beans *drained*
1 tbsp golden caster sugar
sea salt and freshly ground black pepper

Season the lamb with salt and pepper. Heat the oil in a large pan over a high heat and fry the lamb in batches until browned on all sides, then set aside.

Reduce the heat, melt the butter in the pan and throw in the onions. Give them a good stir and let them gently fry for about 15 minutes.

Stir in the garlic and spices, fry for a couple of minutes, then pour in the wine. Scrape the bottom of the pan with a wooden spoon to blend the spices with the wine. Let the mixture simmer for 5 minutes, then return the meat and its juices to the pan. Add the tomatoes and give it all a serious stir. Leave it to gently bubble away for 1½ hours. Check it occasionally to make sure it is not burning or sticking and give it the odd stir. If it begins to look dry, add a little water.

Stir in the beans and sugar to the pan and heat through. Taste and season accordingly with salt and pepper. Remove from the heat and serve with mashed potatoes (see page 187) and spinach that has been briefly boiled and then tossed in a pan with a little cream and nutmeg.

LAMB SHANKS WITH CARAMELISED ONION

This is an extremely popular dish in my house, as it is rich, sweet and tender. It is simple to make and rather satisfying to serve.

TO SERVE FOUR

4 lamb shanks
2 tbsp olive oil
50g/2oz butter
2 large onions *peeled and sliced*
1 tbsp dark brown sugar
2 tbsp sherry vinegar
1 tsp ground ginger
5 cloves

½ tsp each ground turmeric, nutmeg, cumin and coriander
750ml/1¼ pints lamb or chicken stock (*see pages 184 and 185*)
1 handful each dried apricots, prunes, jumbo sultanas and pine nuts
sea salt and freshly ground black pepper

Preheat the oven to 150°C/300°F/gas mark 2.

Season the lamb shanks with salt and pepper. Heat the oil in a large pot with a lid, over a high heat. Brown the shanks on all sides, then put aside on a plate.

Reduce the heat and melt the butter in the pan. Gently fry the onions for about 20 minutes until soft and translucent. Stir in the sugar, vinegar and spices and continue frying for 5–10 minutes, until nicely caramelised.

Stir in the stock, dried fruit and pine nuts. Nestle the shanks into the mixture on their sides and pop into the oven for 2½ hours, turning the shanks halfway through the cooking. Serve with plain basmati rice tossed with plenty of chopped dill, and a crunchy salad.

MEXICAN LAMB

This is a great dish for a crowd. Serve with a big salad, tortillas, dill rice, sour cream, lime wedges and guacamole or simply with rice.

TO SERVE FOUR TO SIX

2 handfuls of dried pinto beans *soaked overnight* or 200g tin of pinto beans *drained*
150g/5oz bacon lardons
2 onions *peeled and sliced*
2 red peppers *cored, seeded and cut into strips*
2 tbsp olive oil
500g/1lb 2oz stewing lamb *cut into chunks and seasoned with salt and pepper*

2 tsp cumin seeds
3 cloves of garlic *peeled and chopped*
1 crushed chipotle chilli (smoked jalapeño), or 1 tsp dried chilli flakes
½ tsp each ground nutmeg and coriander
1 cinnamon stick
400g tin of chopped plum tomatoes
sea salt

If using dried beans, follow the recipe on page 186.

Put the lardons in a large pan on a medium to high heat until the fat begins to run. Add the onions and fry for 10 minutes. Stir in the red peppers and cook for 20 minutes – you want them to gently fry, not steam. Meanwhile, heat the oil in a frying pan over a high heat until smoking. Add the lamb in one layer and leave to fry until nice and brown and a crust has formed on the meat. Turn and fry on the other side. Remove the frying pan from the heat and sprinkle the meat with the cumin seeds. Leave to one side until needed.

Once the peppers and onions are lovely and soft, stir in the garlic, chilli and the rest of the spices and cook through for about 5 minutes. The smell should change once the garlic has cooked – it smells green to start and changes to a smokier smell. Stir in the cooked or tinned beans, followed by the meat, its juices and the cumin seeds. Then add the tomatoes, fill the tomato tin with water and pour this into the pan. Season with salt and give it all a big stir. Leave it on a medium to low heat, stirring every now and then, for 2 hours.

SPANISH LAMB SHOULDER WITH TOMATOES AND OLIVES

I love the scented ingredients of Spain. Paprika, saffron, red peppers and olives make this perfumed dish flavourful and gratifying.

TO SERVE SIX

1.75kg/3¾lb lamb shoulder *bone in*
olive oil
1 tbsp each finely chopped fresh rosemary and thyme
1 Spanish onion *peeled and chopped*
1 red pepper *cored, seeded and sliced*
1 fennel bulb *trimmed and sliced*
2 ribs of celery *cleaned trimmed and chopped*
3 cloves of garlic *peeled and chopped*

1 tsp paprika
400g tin of chopped plum tomatoes
200g/7oz mixed pitted olives
1 pinch of saffron threads
150ml/5fl oz red wine
250ml/9fl oz beef, lamb or chicken stock
(see pages 184 and 185)
sea salt and freshly ground black pepper

Preheat the oven to 220°C/425°F/gas mark 7. Rub the lamb with oil, salt, pepper, rosemary and thyme. Pop in a roasting tray and roast for 20 minutes.

Meanwhile, gently fry the onion, red pepper, fennel and celery in an ovenproof pot with a lid for about 1 hour or until soft, stirring frequently. The pot must be large enough to contain the lamb lying flat.

Reduce the heat of the oven to 150°C/300°F/gas mark 2. Stir the garlic into the onion and cook for a couple of minutes, then add the paprika. Stir through for a couple of minutes, then add the tomatoes, olives and saffron, then the wine and stock. Give it a last stir then submerge the meat into the luscious liquid, cover the pot and pop in the oven for 3 hours.

Remove the meat from the pot and set aside, then boil the sauce to reduce it by half. Slice the meat, place in bowls and spoon the sauce over it. Serve with a lovely crisp green salad.

Vicki Conran's
IRISH STEW

There is always intense excitement in my house when we visit Dad and his wife, Vicki for lunch, and one of the many reasons is Vicki's magnificent cooking. It is always a sensational spread, but more than that it is warm and welcoming. Here is her divine recipe for Irish stew. Vicki recommends cooking the lamb 24 hours before you want to eat it so that when it has cooled, you can lift off the layer of solidified fat from the top. You can also make an elegant version using lamb cutlets and young spring vegetables.

FOR EACH PERSON
— AND IT'S A DISH THAT WORKS VERY WELL MADE IN LARGE QUANTITIES —
YOU WILL NEED:

250g/9oz neck of lamb chops
1 bay leaf
1 medium onion *peeled and roughly sliced*
250g/9oz carrots *peeled and sliced*

250g/9oz old potatoes *peeled and cut into quarters*
1 handful of chopped fresh flat-leaf parsley
sea salt and white pepper

Put the chops into a large covered casserole, cover with cold water and add the bay leaf. Bring to a simmer and cook, covered, on the hob (or in a slow oven 160°C/325°F/gas mark 3), for 2 hours or until the lamb is falling off the bones.

Tip into a bowl and leave in the fridge until cold. Lift off the solidified fat, then remove and discard the bones from the meat. Heat, then strain the cooking liquid. Put the onion, carrots, potatoes, reserved lamb and the strained liquid into a clean casserole and bring to a simmer. Cook gently for about 40 minutes, until the vegetables are tender, then add salt and pepper to taste.

Just before serving in very, very hot deep plates, add the parsley.

LAMB WITH PRESERVED LEMON

You can serve this aromatic and toothsome dish as either a soup or a stew, depending on your mood and the amount of liquid you add. Either way it is quite superb.

TO SERVE FOUR TO SIX

2 handfuls of dried green haricot beans *soaked overnight* or 400g/7oz tinned haricot beans *drained*
2 tbsp olive oil
1kg/2¼lb lamb stewing steak *cut into 3cm/1¼ inch cubes*
50g/2oz butter
2 onions *peeled and chopped*
2 ribs of celery *cleaned, trimmed and chopped*
1 tsp each ground cinnamon, coriander and ginger

1 pinch of saffron threads
½ tsp harissa
2 x 400g tins of plum tomatoes
2 strips of lemon peel *(cut with a potato peeler)*
1 litre/1¾ pints lamb or chicken stock *(see pages 184 and 185)*
peel of 1 preserved lemon *finely chopped*
sea salt and freshly ground black pepper

If using dried beans, drain and thoroughly rinse them, then pour into a large pot with a lid. Cover with plenty of water and place on a medium heat. Bring to the boil and simmer for 30 minutes. Skim off any foam and discard. Change the water, reduce the heat slightly and bring back to the boil. Continue to bubble for a further hour. Drain and put to one side.

Heat the oil in a large pan with a lid, quickly brown the meat on all sides and remove to a plate until needed. Lower the heat and plop the butter into the pan. Stir in the onions and celery and fry until tender – about 20 minutes. Sprinkle in the spices, dollop in the harissa and give it a good stir for a couple of minutes. Continue stirring and pour in the tomatoes. Add the lemon peel and simmer, stirring occasionally, for a further 20 minutes. You should have quite a thick tomato sauce. Stir in the meat, cooked or tinned beans and stock and about 1 litre/1¾ pints of water and leave to plop away at a gentle pace for 2 hours. Check it occasionally and give it a stir and a prod to make sure it is happy and not burning.

Just before serving, stir through the preserved lemon peel, remove the strips of lemon peel and season to taste – the preserved lemon peel is very salty so go easy on the salt. Serve with warm flat bread or naan and French beans with plenty of butter.

PORK SOUPS

PANCETTA AND WHITE BEAN SOUP

BLACK BEAN AND PORK BELLY SOUP

BUTTERNUT SQUASH AND SAUSAGE SOUP

Jean-Christophe Novelli's
GREEN PEA, FOIE GRAS AND PANCETTA CAPPUCCINO

CABBAGE AND PORK POT

PORK STEWS

PORK WITH ASIAN SPICES

LENTILS WITH ITALIAN SAUSAGE

BOSTON BAKED BEANS WITH PORK BELLY

HUNTER'S STEW

CASSOULET

PORK AND PRUNE STEW

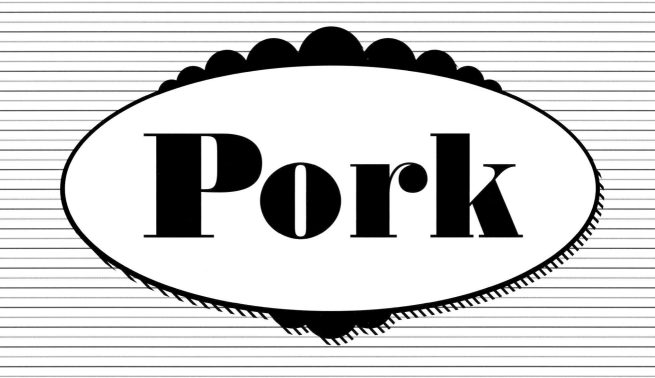

PANCETTA AND WHITE BEAN SOUP

This is a great soup to have plopping away as you potter about with other homey activities. A fantastic standby dish that can be thrown together using stuff in the cupboard.

TO SERVE FOUR

5 handfuls of dried white haricot beans *soaked overnight* or 2 x 400g tins of haricot beans *drained*
2 tbsp olive oil *plus extra to drizzle*
50g/2oz butter
1 large onion *peeled and chopped*
100g/3½oz pancetta *cut into sticks*

3 carrots *peeled and chopped*
3 fat cloves of garlic *peeled and finely chopped*
2 tsp chopped fresh thyme
1 bay leaf
sea salt and freshly ground black pepper

Follow the recipe for cooking beans (see page 186).

Heat the oil and butter in a large pan, and fry the onion, pancetta and carrots for about 15 minutes. Stir in the garlic and thyme and fry for a further 2 minutes. Then pour in the cooked or tinned beans, cover with plenty of water and stir through. Pop in the bay leaf and simmer gently for 3 hours, topping up the water if it starts to dry out.

Season with salt and pepper. Ladle out about half the mixture and whiz in a blender, then return to the pan and stir through.

Serve with a drizzle of olive oil on top and some lovely bread.

BLACK BEAN AND PORK BELLY SOUP

I use ancho chillies in this yummy soup. It is a Mexican pepper with a mild paprika flavour, quite sweet and not very hot. If you can't get hold of them, try paprika or a smoked chilli.

TO SERVE FOUR TO EIGHT

4 handfuls of dried black beans *soaked overnight* or 2 x 400g tins of black beans *drained*
2 tbsp olive oil
500g/1lb 2oz boneless rindless belly of pork
1 large Spanish onion *peeled and chopped*
3 cloves of garlic *peeled and chopped*
2 ancho chillies *cut in half lengthways, seeded and chopped, or 1 tsp crushed dried chilli*

2 tsp ground cumin
400g tin of peeled, chopped tomatoes
1 tbsp raw cane sugar
250g tin of sweetcorn kernels *drained*
1 handful of chopped fresh coriander
soured cream, to serve
sea salt and freshly ground black pepper

If using dried beans, drain and thoroughly rinse them then pour into a large pot with a lid. Cover with plenty of water and place on a medium heat. Bring to the boil and simmer for 30 minutes. Skim off any foam and discard. Change the water, reduce the heat slightly and bring back to the boil. Continue to bubble for a further 1 hour. Drain and put to one side.

Heat the oil in a large pan on a medium heat and drop in the pork, fat side down. Fry for 10 minutes, then turn to brown the other side, and remove to a plate. Throw the onion into the pan and fry for 10–15 minutes until soft, stirring every now and again. Stir in the garlic, chillies and cumin and continue frying for a couple of minutes, then pour in the tomatoes. Stir in the sugar, season with salt and pepper and simmer for a further 20 minutes, or until you have a thick tomato sauce.

Stir the cooked or tinned beans into the tomatoes, pop the pork back in the pan and cover with water. Bring to the boil and simmer gently for 2 hours. Remove the meat from the pan and slice into chunks. Blend about four ladlefuls of the beans to a purée, then stir back into the pan with the meat, corn and coriander. Season to taste, heat through and serve with a big dollop of soured cream on top. This is lovely served with salad, sliced avocado, lime wedges and radishes.

BUTTERNUT SQUASH AND SAUSAGE SOUP

This is a favourite with my kids. It can be made with all sorts of roast veg, but the sweetness and texture of the squash are great as a main ingredient. Slice the sausages as you like or leave them out for a veggie dish.

TO SERVE EIGHT TO TEN

7 juniper berries
1½ tsp caraway seeds
1 butternut squash *peeled, seeded and chopped*
2 small sweet potatoes *peeled and chopped*
2 small parsnips *peeled and chopped*

2 carrots *peeled and chopped*
2 tbsp olive oil
6 pure pork sausages
sea salt and freshly ground black pepper

Preheat the oven to 190°C/375°F/gas mark 5.

Crush the juniper berries and caraway seeds with a pestle and mortar. Put all the veg, the oil, spices and seasoning in a large roasting pan and mix with your hands until the veg are well coated with the oil and spices. Pop into the oven for 45 minutes or until the vegetables are golden and soft, turning over once halfway through cooking, to ensure they are evenly roasted. Remove from the oven and leave to cool. Meanwhile, fry the sausages in a large pan.

Purée the vegetables with enough water to give a lovely soupy consistency and season to taste. Remove the sausages from the pan and slice them. Pour the soup into the pan, add the sausages, stir through, then reheat.

Jean-Christophe Novelli's
GREEN PEA, FOIE GRAS AND PANCETTA CAPPUCCINO

It is always a pleasure to see Jean-Christophe's smiling face. Here he transforms the humble pea into light foaming soup with crisp pancetta and silky foie gras. Bon appetit!

TO SERVE FOUR TO SIX

25ml/1fl oz olive oil
1 small onion *peeled and diced*
1 shallot *peeled and diced*
450g/1lb fresh or frozen peas
800ml/1 pint 7fl oz light chicken stock
1 clove of garlic *peeled*
1 pinch of caster sugar
6 sprigs of fresh garden mint
sea salt and freshly ground black pepper

For the garnish (see Tips)
1 x 2cm/¾inch thickness foie gras divided into 4 *seasoned with salt, pepper and a little fine sugar*
30g/1¼oz lardons of pancetta
1 clove garlic, *peeled and chopped*
1 sprig of fresh thyme
olive oil

For the cappuccino topping
6 tbsp full-fat milk or crème fraîche
cep powder (see Tips)

Heat the oil in a large pan, add the onion and shallot and sweat gently until soft but not coloured. Add the peas and stock and bring quickly to the boil. Cook until the peas are slightly soft to the touch – about 1 minute.

Place the mix into a blender and mix for 30 seconds, then allow to stand for another 30 seconds. Add the garlic, salt and pepper, sugar and the mint and blend until totally smooth, or pass through a fine sieve if the soup is too coarse. Keep the soup hot while you prepare the garnish and milk foam.

For the garnish, sear the slices of foie gras in a very hot pan for a few seconds only until crispy on the outside and soft in the middle. In the same pan, dry-fry the pancetta with pepper, garlic and thyme and a little more oil, drain and allow to cool and crisp up.

For the cappuccino topping, bring the milk to the boil or warm the crème fraîche. If you have a cappuccino frother, froth up the warm milk to a foam (or alternatively, whisk the warm crème fraîche using a hand blender).

To serve pour the soup into individual warm soup terrines or coffee cups, spoon a little of the milk foam or crème fraîche on top and finish with a slice of foie gras, crispy pancetta and a dusting of cep powder for the cappuccino effect.

TIPS

- Frozen peas taste just as good as fresh and usually contain more vitamins and minerals and are virtually cooked to start with.
- This soup can be made similarly with broad beans, asparagus, spinach or watercress and served chilled in the summer like a vichyssoise.
- Vegetable stock can be substituted for the chicken stock.
- Chicken livers or even mushrooms can be substituted for the foie gras.
- Most supermarkets and delicatessens will stock pancetta but if you can't find it good-quality dry-cured bacon is a useful substitute.
- Cep or wild mushroom powder can be made at home by grinding bought dried ceps or wild mushrooms in a grinder until a fine dusting powder results. This may take a little time but is well worth the effort.

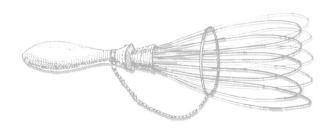

CABBAGE AND PORK POT

A few basic ingredients make a calming and reviving soup. It is gorgeous to behold and nectar for the taste buds.

TO SERVE FOUR

2 tbsp olive oil
50g/2oz butter
1 onion *peeled and chopped*
1 leek *cleaned, trimmed and chopped*
4 carrots *peeled and chopped*

550g/1¼lb cured smoked pork loin
½ Savoy cabbage *trimmed, cored and sliced*
1 handful of chopped fresh flat-leaf parsley
sea salt and freshly ground black pepper

Heat the oil and butter in a large pan, and dump in all the vegetables except the cabbage. Season with pepper and fry until soft – about 20 minutes.

Add the pork to the pot and cover with water. Bring to gentle simmer and cook for 1 hour. Remove the meat from the pot, throw in the cabbage and cook for 5 minutes. Slice the meat into finger-sized pieces and plop back into the soup with the parsley.

Season to taste and serve once the cabbage is cooked.

PORK WITH ASIAN SPICES

This is a real melt-in-the-mouth dish. The spices and ginger give it a wonderful fragrance.

TO SERVE FOUR TO SIX

olive oil
50g/2oz butter
2 red onions *peeled and sliced*
1kg/2¼lb boneless pork loin
cut into 3cm/1¼inch cubes
1 tbsp cornflour
50ml/2fl oz sherry

3 cloves of garlic *peeled and chopped*
2 tsp five-spice powder
1 walnut-sized piece of fresh root ginger *peeled and chopped*
4 tbsp light soy sauce
sea salt and freshly ground black pepper

Heat 1 tablespoon of oil and the butter in a large pan on a medium heat. Gently fry the onions, stirring frequently, for 15 minutes.

Meanwhile, coat the meat in the cornflour and season with salt and pepper. Add a glug of oil to another pan and fry the pork in batches until nicely browned all over. Transfer the meat to a bowl and set aside. Deglaze the pan with the sherry and a little water. Pour this sauce over the meat.

Go back to the onion pan and stir in the garlic, five-spice and ginger and fry for a couple of minutes. Add the meat, sauce and soy sauce to the pan. Stir in enough water to just cover the meat, then bring to a gentle tremble of a boil and cook for 2 hours, stirring from time to time.

Serve with stir-fried noodles or egg fried rice.

LENTILS WITH ITALIAN SAUSAGE

The cotechino is a most delicious, large Italian boiling sausage that goes exceptionally well with lentils. At New Year in Italy, sausage and lentils are eaten to bring health and prosperity; the fatness of the sausage represents health, the lentils prosperity because they resemble little coins.

TO SERVE FOUR

knob of butter	1 tsp finely chopped rosemary
glug of olive oil	500g/1lb 2oz Puy lentils
1 red onion *peeled and chopped*	1 chicken stock cube
2 small carrots *peeled and chopped*	1 bay leaf
2 celery ribs *cleaned and peeled*	1 cotechino *cut into 1cm/½ inch pieces*
1 tsp finely chopped fresh thyme	sea salt and freshly ground black pepper

Melt the butter in a large frying pan, add the olive oil and gently fry the onion, carrots, celery, thyme and rosemary with a good grind of black pepper for 20 minutes, or until soft.

Stir in the lentils, stock cube and bay leaf and cover with water. Season with salt and leave to simmer for 45 minutes, adding more water if necessary.

Cook the cotechino as directed on the packet instructions then stir into the lentils. Serve with bread and a green salad on the side.

BOSTON BAKED BEANS WITH PORK BELLY

Boston is known as 'Beantown', because this dish has been one of the most favoured there since colonial days, when molasses was America's primary sweetener. Boston used to be a huge producer of molasses, due to the local rum industry (sugar cane was grown in the West Indies and shipped to Boston to be made into rum). The Great Molasses Flood is probably the stickiest disaster in history: in 1919 a massive flood of molasses broke out of a storage tank and swept through a large part of the city, wreaking havoc and causing dozens of deaths. It is said that on hot days you can still smell the molasses seeping out of the pavements.

TO SERVE FOUR TO SIX

10 handfuls of dried white haricot beans *soaked overnight*
2 small onions *peeled and chopped*
2 cloves of garlic *peeled and finely chopped*
2 tsp mustard powder
1 scant tbsp salt

1–2 tbsp molasses *depending on how much you like the flavour*
1 tbsp raw cane sugar
1 good grind of fresh black pepper
500g/1lb 2oz piece boneless, rindless belly of pork

Drain and thoroughly rinse the beans, then pour into a large pot with a lid. Cover with plenty of water and place on a medium heat. Bring to the boil and simmer for 30 minutes. Skim off any foam and discard. Change the water, reduce the heat slightly and bring back to the boil. Continue to bubble for a further 1 hour.

Preheat the oven to 120°C/250°F/gas mark ½.

Make sure there is enough liquid to cover the beans, then stir in all the ingredients, lastly embedding the pork into the beans. Cover with a lid and pop in the oven for 8 hours. Excellent with a fry-up, with extra black pudding, please. Or with a baked potato and salad. Something fresh and crunchy.

HUNTER'S STEW

This is a real peasant dish, packed with all sorts of porky bits and wonderful big earthy flavours. Enjoy with a slab of really good bread. It is not so pretty, but by God is it tasty.

TO SERVE EIGHT TO TEN

2 tbsp olive oil
1kg/2¼lb boneless pork shoulder *cut into 3cm/1¼ inch cubes*
500g/1lb 2oz boneless, rindless belly of pork *cut into 1cm/½ inch cubes*
125g/4oz Spanish chorizo *skinned and cut into 1cm/½ inch cubes*
3 onions *peeled and sliced*
250g/9oz button mushrooms *sliced*
3 fat cloves of garlic *peeled and chopped*

2 tsp caraway seeds *slightly crushed in a pestle and mortar*
1 handful of chopped fresh marjoram
3 tbsp tomato purée
1 small head of Savoy cabbage *trimmed, cored and sliced*
400g/14oz Polish boiling sausage *skinned and sliced*
330ml bottle or can of Golden ale or lager
2 tbsp cornflour
sea salt and freshly ground black pepper

Heat the oil on a high heat in a very large pan with a lid. Season the pork shoulder with salt and pepper and fry in the oil in batches until the cubes have a nice brown crust. Remove to a plate. Fry the pork belly and chorizo in the pan until beginning to crisp, then set aside with the pork shoulder .

Dump the onions into the pan and fry, stirring frequently, for about 20 minutes. Throw in the mushrooms and continue cooking for a further 5 minutes, then stir in the garlic, caraway seeds and marjoram and cook for 2 minutes. Stir in the tomato purée, cabbage, reserved meat and the boiling sausage and pour in the beer and enough water to almost cover the meat. Season with salt and pepper. Stir well and cover with a lid, leaving a little crack for the steam to escape, and leave to gently stew for 1 hour.

Mix the cornflour with about 5 tablespoons of water, stir into the stew and simmer to thicken. Serve with noodles, or a hefty slab of great bread.

CASSOULET

This dish from south-west France has peasant roots and a myriad of versions. Mine is simple, but the result is rich and totally gorgeous.

TO SERVE SIX TO EIGHT

500g/1lb 2oz dried white haricot beans *soaked overnight*
2 tbsp olive oil
500g/1lb 2oz piece boneless, rindless belly of pork
400g/14oz Toulouse sausages *or other pure pork sausages*
250g/9oz pancetta *cut into sticks*
2 onions *peeled and chopped*
2 ribs of celery *cleaned, trimmed and chopped*
2 carrots *peeled and chopped*

4 fat cloves of garlic *peeled and sliced*
1 tsp each finely chopped fresh thyme and rosemary
6 ripe tomatoes *peeled, seeded and cut into quarters (see page 121)*
2 bay leaves
2 preserved duck legs *(confit) from a jar or tin, fat removed*
20.5cm/8 inch piece of stale baguette
sea salt and freshly ground black pepper

Follow the recipe for cooking beans (see page 186). Heat the oil in a large pan with a lid and fry the various porky bits until browned, then remove them to a plate, reduce the heat then fry the onions, celery and carrots in the fat until soft – about 20 minutes. Add the garlic, thyme and rosemary and stir through for a couple of minutes. Pour the tomatoes into the vegetable mixture and cook down to a thick sauce – this should take 15–20 minutes.

Preheat the oven to 150°C/300°F/gas mark 2. Season the vegetable mixture with salt and pepper, then start assembling the whole dish. Choose a nice big ovenproof pot! Stir the beans, bay leaves, pancetta and about 500ml/18fl oz of water into the veg, then bury the duck legs, sausages and pork in the beans. Bring to a gentle boil, cover with the lid and pop in the oven for 1½ hours. Once the time is up, blitz the baguette in a food processor then sprinkle over the cassoulet. Return it to the oven for another 30 minutes, uncovered, so that the breadcrumbs crisp up.

PORK AND PRUNE STEW

I am a big fan of pork and prunes together. They seem to work however they are served, whether as Devils on Horseback (bacon-wrapped stuffed prunes) or as a lovely loin rolled and stuffed with prunes. This is no exception.

TO SERVE FOUR

4 tbsp olive oil
500g/1lb 2oz boneless leg of pork
cut into 4cm x 2cm/1½ x ¾ inch strips
50g/2oz butter
1 large onion *peeled and sliced*
3 cloves of garlic *peeled and chopped*
1 tsp each sea salt and freshly ground black pepper

75g/3oz demerara sugar
½ tsp finely chopped fresh marjoram
¼ tsp finely chopped fresh thyme
500ml/18fl oz dry cider
200g/7oz stoned, ready-to-eat prunes
1 small handful of chopped fresh sage leaves

Heat the oil in a large pan with a lid over a high heat, until softened. Be careful not to let the onion and garlic brown.

Return the pork to the pan and stir in the sugar, marjoram and thyme. Allow the sugar to dissolve, then add the cider, prunes and sage. Put on the lid and simmer for 1 hour. Check occasionally to ensure it is not sticking to the pan and stir it through from time to time.

After 1 hour remove the lid and simmer for a further 45 minutes to allow the sauce to thicken. I like to serve this with purple sprouting broccoli and roast potatoes.

GAME SOUPS

PHEASANT CONSOMMÉ WITH BABY VEGETABLES

Richard Corrigan's
SPLIT LENTIL SOUP WITH BRAISED HARE

HIGHLAND GAMES

RIBOLLITA

GAME STEWS

VENISON AND ROOT VEGETABLES

VENISON WITH PORT AND PLUMS

IRISH RABBIT STEW

Chris Galvin's
DAUBE OF VENISON WITH QUINCE AND CHESTNUTS

PHEASANT WITH RED CABBAGE

RED DUCK CURRY

PHEASANT AND SAUSAGE STEW

Game

PHEASANT CONSOMMÉ WITH BABY VEGETABLES

I think pheasant makes some of the best stock or broth, and here, consommé. You can use a couple of whole birds that are a bit old and too tough for eating instead of just the carcasses, to make the consommé. However it is made, this is a truly delightful soup.

TO SERVE FOUR

For the consommé
4 fresh pheasant carcasses
½ bottle of white wine
1 bay leaf
1 small bunch of fresh flat-leaf parsley
2 ribs of celery *cleaned and trimmed*
3 carrots *peeled*
1 leek *cleaned, trimmed and cut in half*

For the baby spring vegetables
12 baby carrots *peeled*
8 baby spring onions *trimmed, cut in half lengthways*
8 baby courgettes *trimmed, cut in half lengthways*
1 handful each tiny peas and broad beans
sea salt

Put all the ingredients for the consommé in a ginormous pot, cover with water and simmer extremely gently for 2 hours.

Strain the contents of the pan through a muslin-lined sieve (or a clean tea towel will do) and discard the bones and veg. Clean the pan, pour the broth back into it and boil vigorously to reduce until you have just over 1 litre/1¾ pints – this intensifies the flavours. Skim off as much fat as possible.

Bring back to the boil, season with salt to taste, then start adding the vegetables. First cook the carrots and onions for 5 minutes, then add the rest of the veg, bring back to the boil and boil for 2 minutes. Ladle the vegetables into bowls, then pour the consommé over them and serve.

Richard Corrigan's
SPLIT LENTIL SOUP WITH BRAISED HARE

I have long been a fan of Richard's sublime cooking. He really has a delicate touch; in this recipe tender hare nestles in a bowl of vegetable and leek soup.

TO SERVE FOUR

For the soup
350g/12oz split lentils *soaked in cold water overnight*
50g/2oz butter
2 carrots *peeled and finely chopped*
2 ribs of celery *cleaned, trimmed and finely chopped*
1 leek *cleaned, trimmed and finely chopped*
2 sprigs of fresh thyme
1 clove of garlic *peeled and crushed*
900ml/1½ pints chicken stock
splash of Pedro Ximinez vinegar
sea salt and freshly ground black pepper

For the hare
2 hare legs
plain flour *seasoned with salt and pepper, for dusting*
1 tbsp oil
1 carrot *peeled and finely chopped*
2 ribs of celery *cleaned, trimmed and finely chopped*

1 onion *peeled and finely chopped*
1 leek *cleaned, trimmed and finely chopped*
knob of butter
2 sprigs of fresh thyme
1 clove of garlic *peeled*
100ml/3½fl oz red wine
600ml/1 pint veal or chicken stock
150ml/5fl oz chicken stock *(see page 185)*

For the garnish
5g/¼oz butter
1 carrot *peeled and cut into dice*
1 rib of celery *cleaned, trimmed and cut into dice*
1 onion *peeled and cut into dice*
1 leek *cleaned, trimmed and cut into dice*
50g/2oz cooked split lentils
1 tsp chopped fresh flat-leaf parsley

First make the soup. Drain the lentils and put to one side. Heat the butter in a heavy pan, then add all the vegetables and cook until softened without colouring. Add the thyme, garlic and lentils to the pan. Cover with the stock and cook until the lentils are soft.

Next, cook the hare. Roll the hare in the seasoned flour and colour in a frying pan with the oil. Remove and leave to one side. Place all the vegetables in a heavy-based pan with the butter.

Cook until soft, then add the thyme, garlic and wine. Reduce by half, then add the veal and chicken stocks. Add the hare legs and braise for 2 hours. Leave to cool in the liquor. When cool, remove the hare from the pan and take off the meat from the bone. Strain the liquid and heat to reduce by three-quarters. Return the hare to the pan, cover the pan to keep it warm and leave to one side.

Using a blender, blitz the soup and pass through a fine sieve. Season and add a splash of Pedro Ximinez vinegar.

For the garnish, cook all the vegetables separately in the butter until tender, then combine. Add the lentils and parsley.

To serve, warm the soup. Scatter a spoonful of garnish into each bowl and add 3–4 pieces of hare in each. Serve the hot soup on the side.

HIGHLAND GAMES

The Scottish Highland Games go back further than historical records, but nowadays the Games are like a mini Scottish Olympics, with huge, muscular men in kilts throwing hammers and tossing humungous cabers, which are very long and heavy poles that are thrown so hard that they flip over. Obviously our kilted athletes need a hearty, meaty soup. So, here it is. Och aye the noo!

TO SERVE EIGHT

500g/1lb 2oz venison *cut into roughly 5cm/2 inch pieces*
500g/1lb 2oz prepared pheasant *cut into roughly 5cm/2 inch pieces*
2 tbsp plain flour
1 tsp each finely chopped fresh rosemary and thyme
2 tbsp olive oil
50g/2oz butter
2 ribs of celery *cleaned, trimmed and chopped*

1 leek *cleaned, trimmed and chopped*
1 potato the size of your fist *peeled and cubed*
1 red onion *peeled and chopped*
2 carrots *peeled and chopped*
1 tsp each ground cinnamon and ginger
¼ tsp ground nutmeg
1.5 litres/2½ pints stock *(pheasant is best, but chicken or beef is fine; see pages 184 and 185)*
sea salt and freshly ground black pepper

Put the meat, flour and chopped herbs into a bowl and season with salt and pepper. Stir through with your hands until all the meat is coated. Cook the meat in batches. Heat the oil in a large pot and drop enough pieces of meat into the pan to cover in one layer. Fry until crisp and browned, then turn over and brown the other side. When all the meat is done, remove to a plate and put to one side.

Turn down the heat, add the butter to the pot and drop in all the veg. Cook until softened, stirring often, for about 15 minutes. Stir in the spices for a couple of minutes, then pour in the stock and bring to the boil. Simmer for 30 minutes, or until the veg are very tender.

Meanwhile, chop the meat into 1cm/½ inch cubes. Take the soup off the heat and cool a little, then whiz in a blender until smooth. Season to taste, stir in the meat and heat through. Serve with tasty rolls. Best eaten to the sound of bagpipes.

RIBOLLITA

This is a Tuscan soup with wonderful earthy flavours. I have added the pigeon breasts on top since it is one of my favourite meats and complements the soup wonderfully. I recommend the use of a knife and fork for this one.

TO SERVE SIX TO EIGHT

3 tbsp olive oil, plus extra for drizzling
100g/3½oz pancetta *cut into little sticks*
50g/2oz butter
1 medium onion *peeled and finely chopped*
2 medium carrots *peeled and finely chopped*
2 ribs of celery *cleaned, trimmed and finely chopped*
1 leek, *cleaned trimmed and finely chopped*
2 fat cloves of garlic *peeled and chopped*
1 tsp fresh finely chopped rosemary
½ tsp chilli flakes

1.5 litres/2½ pints chicken stock *(see page 185)*
400g tin of pinto, cannellini or navy beans *with liquid*
1 head of cavolo nero *leaves only, cleaned and chopped*
6 tomatoes *peeled, seeded and cut into quarters* *(see page 121)*
1 pigeon breast per person
1 slice of ciabatta per person *toasted*
a few fresh thyme leaves *to serve*
sea salt and freshly ground black pepper

Heat a tablespoon of olive oil in a large pot and fry the pancetta until it browns slightly and the fat runs out. Sling in another tablespoon of oil and dollop in the butter. Add the onion, carrots, celery and leek to the pan and gently fry for 15 minutes, stirring from time to time. Stir in the garlic, rosemary and chilli and continue to cook for a couple of minutes. Pour in the stock and beans, and stir in the cavolo nero and tomatoes. Bring to the boil and season to taste. Boil gently for 30 minutes.

Ladle out 3 spoonfuls of the soup and blend to a purée, then return it to the pot. Top the soup up with a little water if it is looking dry. Meanwhile, towards the end of the cooking time, make the toast. Season the pigeon breasts and fry in the remaining oil for about 4 minutes on each side, or until browned on the outside, but still a little pink inside. Remove to a board and leave to sit for about 5 minutes, then cut into 1cm/½ inch thick slices.

Ladle the soup into bowls, lay a slice of toast on top and place a pigeon breast onto the toast. Sprinkle over a few thyme leaves, drizzle with oil and serve.

VENISON AND ROOT VEGETABLES

A glorious warming stew, perfect served with a baked potato or mash (see page 187).

TO SERVE SIX

2 tbsp olive oil
50g/2oz butter
2 onions *peeled and chopped*
2 tbsp sherry vinegar
2 tbsp redcurrant jelly
1.5kg/3lb 5oz venison shoulder, cut into *4cm/1½ inch cubes*
1 tbsp plain flour *seasoned with salt and pepper*

3 large carrots *peeled and chopped*
½ head of celeriac *peeled and chopped*
2 parsnips *peeled and chopped*
2 tsp finely chopped fresh rosemary
500ml/18fl oz beef stock *(see page 184)*
2 tbsp Worcestershire sauce
300ml/10fl oz red wine
sea salt

Heat half the oil and the butter in a large pan with a lid and gently fry the onions for about 10 minutes. Stir in the vinegar and redcurrant jelly and bubble for 15 minutes, stirring frequently. Preheat the oven to 150°C/300°F/gas mark 2.

Meanwhile, coat the meat in the seasoned flour. Heat the remaining oil in a large frying pan and fry the venison in batches until browned.

Add the rest of the veg and the rosemary to the onions and cook, stirring, for 5 minutes. Plop the browned venison in with the veg and any remaining flour, and stir in the stock and Worcestershire sauce. Return to the frying pan – deglaze with the wine, boiling and stirring in all the gubbins, then pour into the pan with the meat and veg.

Season with salt and give it a last loving stir. Then pop the lid on and slide into the oven for 2 hours.

VENISON WITH PORT AND PLUMS

The tart plums in this rich stew contrast superbly with the sweetness of the port. If you would rather make it with red wine, add half a tablespoon of raw cane sugar to balance the tartness of the plums.

TO SERVE SIX

1kg/2¼lb venison shoulder, leg or neck *cut into 4cm/1½ inch cubes*

For the marinade
½ bottle of port
8 juniper berries *crushed*
2 bay leaves
4 cloves of garlic *peeled and crushed*
½ red onion *peeled and sliced*
2 tbsp olive oil
sea salt and freshly ground black pepper

For the stew
2 tbsp olive oil
1 tbsp plain flour *seasoned with salt and pepper*
150g/5oz bacon lardons
1½ red onions *peeled and chopped*
1 cinnamon stick
5 large unripe (so they are slightly sour) red plums *cut in half and stoned*

Mix all the ingredients for the marinade in a bowl. Add the venison and stir to coat, then transfer to an airtight container and leave to infuse for 4 hours, or overnight, in the fridge. Strain off the marinade and reserve, but throw out the onion and bay leaves.

Heat the oil in a large pot with a lid over a medium to high heat. Coat the venison in the flour and fry it in batches until it has just browned on the outside. Once browned, keep the meat to one side. Fry the lardons in the same pot until they start to brown, then reduce the heat. Add the onions and continue to fry for 10 minutes or until the onions are soft. Don't forget to stir them now and again, so they don't burn or get stuck to the pan.

Pour the reserved marinade into the pot and mix it in thoroughly, scraping up all the gubbins stuck to the bottom of the pan. Allow it to bubble away for about 5 minutes until it thickens. Throw in the meat, any juice and the cinnamon stick. Simmer very gently for 1½ hours. Stir in the plums and continue to cook for a further 30 minutes. Serve with roast root vegetables and pommes dauphinoise (see page 188).

IRISH RABBIT STEW

Stobhach Gaelach, or Irish Stew, is traditionally made with lamb or mutton. The rabbit makes a wonderful alternative to lamb as it becomes tender, succulent and tasty.

TO SERVE SIX TO EIGHT

1 prepared rabbit *cut into eight pieces*
1 tbsp plain flour *seasoned with salt and pepper*
2 tbsp olive oil
2 leeks white parts only *cleaned, trimmed and sliced*
2 large carrots *peeled and chopped*
2 baking potatoes *peeled and cut into 2cm/¾ inch cubes*

500ml/18fl oz chicken stock *(see page 185)* or vegetable stock
1½ tsp chopped fresh thyme
1 handful of chopped fresh flat-leaf parsley
sea salt and freshly ground black pepper

Preheat the oven to 180°F/350°F/gas mark 4.

Coat the rabbit pieces in the seasoned flour. Heat the oil in a large pot with a lid and quickly brown the rabbit on all sides – do this in a couple of batches.

Put all the ingredients except the parsley into the pot and season well. Bring to the boil, pop on the lid and transfer to the oven for 1½ hours.

Stir through the parsley and season to taste. Serve with cabbage, red or green.

Chris Galvin's
DAUBE OF VENISON WITH QUINCE AND CHESTNUTS

Chris is an inspiration to me: charming, humble and incredibly talented.

TO SERVE FOUR

1kg/2¼lb venison shoulder *sinew removed*
500ml/18fl oz red wine
250ml/9fl oz port
1 rib of celery *cleaned, trimmed and cut into large dice*
½ onion *peeled and cut into large dice*
3 cloves of garlic *peeled*
1 sprig of fresh thyme
2 litres/3½ pints veal stock
2 knobs of cold butter

50g/2oz trompette mushroom
25g/1oz clarified butter
1 quince
50g/2oz runny honey
10g/¼oz sugar
50g/2oz butter
12 chestnuts *roasted and skinned*
chopped fresh flat-leaf parsley

Marinate the venison in the alcohol along with the vegetables, garlic and thyme. Leave for 24 hours. Preheat the oven to 150°C/300°F/gas mark 2. Strain the marinade and place the venison and vegetables to one side and reserve the liquid. Brown off the venison and vegetables in a very hot frying pan. Boil the marinade until reduced by half then pass through a fine sieve. Meanwhile, boil the veal stock until reduced by half. Put to one side.

Transfer the meat, vegetables and marinade to a braising pan. Pour in the boiling veal stock, bring back to the boil, cover with tin foil and place in the oven for about 2 hours or until the meat is tender. Allow to cool in the cooking liquor. Pick out the venison from the vegetables and reserve. Strain the liquid through a fine sieve. To make the sauce, reduce the cooking liquor until sauce consistency, then whisk in a couple of knobs of cold butter.

Peel the quince and cut into wedges. Place in a pan with the honey and sugar and cook until golden and tender. Warm the venison and chestnuts in the sauce, spoon into bowl plates and add the hot quince to each. Melt the butter in a small pan and gently fry the mushrooms. Pop on top of the venison, sprinkle with parsley and serve.

PHEASANT WITH RED CABBAGE

Whenever I have red cabbage I always wonder why I don't have it more often as I love it. This red cabbage can also be made without the pheasant. It is great with any roast, especially duck and goose.

TO SERVE FOUR TO SIX

2 tbsp olive oil
2 prepared pheasants *each cut into eight pieces*
200g/7oz diced pancetta *diced*
2 red onions *peeled and chopped*
1 large red cabbage *cored and sliced*
1 cooking apple
300ml/10fl oz red wine

1 bay leaf
7 juniper berries *crushed*
1½ tbsp raw cane sugar
2 strips of orange peel and the juice of 1 orange
500ml/18fl oz beef stock *(see page 184)*
sea salt and freshly ground black pepper

Preheat the oven to 150°C/300°F/gas mark 2.

Heat the oil in a large pan with a lid on a medium heat. Season the pheasants with salt and pepper and brown in the oil in batches, then remove to a plate. Throw the pancetta into the pan and fry for 5 minutes. Jiggle the dice about a bit so the fat runs out and they begin to crisp but don't burn. Remove from the pan and keep aside with the pheasant.

Turn down the heat, stir in the onions and cook until soft – about 10 minutes. Stir in the cabbage. Peel, core and cut the apple into bite-sized pieces. Stir into the pan and cook for about 5 minutes, stirring to coat everything with the bacon fat. Pour in the wine, then stir in the bay leaf, juniper berries, sugar, orange peel and juice, and season with salt and a good grind of black pepper.

Cover the pan, pop it in the oven and cook for 1 hour. Remove from the oven and stir in the meat and stock. Return to the oven, uncovered, for a further hour. Serve with baked potatoes.

RED DUCK CURRY

Be careful when handling chillies, as their volatile oil can burn your eyes or any delicate area if you touch them. Wear rubber gloves, or wash your hands several times in cold water with soap after handling them. When we were kids we had a cottage in France. In the summer, family and friends came to stay and everyone cooked and played in the big open-plan kitchen. I remember one of my dad's friends running out of the bathroom hopping about like Rumpelstiltskin. It turned out he had been chopping some particularly potent chillies and had then gone for a pee. Poor Kaz was in such pain, but we all laughed so hard.

TO SERVE SIX

4 duck breasts
a drizzle of olive oil
1 red onion *peeled and sliced*
2 tbsp red curry paste (*see below*)
1 acorn squash *cut into chunks and seeded*
400ml tin of coconut milk
30 cherry tomatoes
1 handful of chopped fresh coriander or basil
sea salt and freshly ground black pepper

For the red curry paste
1 handful of dried shrimps
5 hot little chillies *cut in half lengthways and seeded*
5 cloves of garlic *peeled*
2 sticks of lemon grass *chopped*
10 small spring onions *trimmed and chopped*
2 heaped tsp shrimp paste
1 tsp tamarind concentrate
5 kaffir lime leaves *chopped*
1 tbsp raw cane sugar
1 walnut-sized piece of fresh root ginger *peeled and chopped*
75ml/3fl oz sesame oil

Put all the ingredients for the red curry paste except the sesame oil into a blender and whiz away. Slowly drizzle in the oil until you get a sloppy red paste. (The paste can be frozen or kept in the fridge for 3 weeks. It can also be used with chicken, beef, seafood or vegetables.)

Score the duck fat with a sharp knife. Heat a tiny bit of olive oil in a large pan. The oil is just to stop the duck sticking to the pan – the duck will produce copious amounts of fat from the

cont.

cont.

skin. Place the duck, skin side down, in the pan and fry for about 10 minutes on a medium heat, or until the skin is brown and crisp and has rendered most of the fat. Turn, and brown the other side for 3 minutes. Remove from the pan and set aside.

Pour most of the oil out of the pan into a heatproof bowl (this can be kept for frying potatoes). Fry the onion until it becomes soft – about 10 minutes. Then add half the curry paste and continue to fry for a further 5 minutes. You can save the rest of the paste for use at a later date .

Stir in the squash until coated in curry paste and pour in a little of the coconut milk. Amalgamate the rest of the coconut milk into the mixture, slowly adding a little more and stirring through until you have a lovely smooth, rich sauce. Leave to bubble away for about 25 minutes, stirring from time to time.

Meanwhile, cut the duck into slices as thick as your thumb, then stir them into the curry with the tomatoes. Heat through for 5 minutes. Stir in the coriander or basil and serve with basmati rice and buttered French beans.

PHEASANT AND SAUSAGE STEW

An excellent dish that can also be made with left-over roast game birds, such as partridge, grouse and quail. Cook in exactly the same way except omit the pheasant, adding the meat at the end, then heating through.

TO SERVE FOUR

2 tbsp olive oil
1 prepared fat pheasant
3 excellent sausages *skins removed*
1 onion *peeled and chopped*
1 leek *cleaned, trimmed and chopped*
1 rib of celery *cleaned, trimmed and chopped*
2 carrots *peeled and chopped*
250g/9oz button mushrooms *quartered*

½ bottle of red wine
4 dollops of Worcestershire sauce
2 bay leaves
1 tsp ground coriander
1 tsp cornflour
100ml/3½fl oz chicken stock *(see page 185)*
1½ tbsp golden caster sugar
sea salt and freshly ground black pepper

Heat the oil in a large pot on a high heat. Season the pheasant with salt and pepper. Quickly brown it all over in the oil, then take it out of the pot and put it on a plate for later.

Roll the sausage meat into balls a bit smaller than walnuts. Reduce the heat, then cook them in the oil, rolling them around until they are nicely browned and cooked through. Set them aside. Reduce the heat. Add all the chopped vegetables to the pan and stir, then gently fry for 15 minutes. Pour in the wine and Worcestershire sauce and add the herbs. Put the pheasant in the pan on its side, cover with a lid and simmer for 15 minutes. Turn the pheasant over and simmer for a further 15 minutes. Remove the pheasant from the pan and leave to cool for 10 minutes. Keep cooking the vegetables for another 10 minutes until the wine has reduced. Cut the pheasant meat from the carcass into bite-sized chunks.

Mix the cornflour into a little of the chicken stock, add to the pot with the rest of the stock and simmer for 5 minutes to thicken, then remove from the heat. Stir the pheasant meat, sugar and sausage balls into the stew and heat through.

Serve with mashed potatoes (see page 187) and Savoy cabbage.

CHICKEN SOUPS

MY SOOTHING CHICKEN AND NOODLE SOUP

FRESH PASTA

CREAM OF CHICKEN SOUP WITH TARRAGON

MEXICAN CHICKEN SOUP – CALDO DE POLLO

MUM'S CHICKEN SOUP

(JEWISH PENICILLIN) SOOTHING MATZO BALL SOUP

Ching-he Huang's
HOT AND SOUR CHICKEN AND EXOTIC MUSHROOM SOUP

CHICKEN STEWS

COQ AU VIN

Caroline Conran's
CHICKEN AND MUSHROOM STEW

FRAGRANT CHICKEN STEW

CHICKEN, CHORIZO AND BUTTERBEAN STEW

CARIBBEAN COCONUT CURRY

LEMON CHICKEN WITH SPINACH

CHICKEN CURRY FOR LITTLE CHICKENS

SLOPPY, SPICY, RED CHICKEN STEW

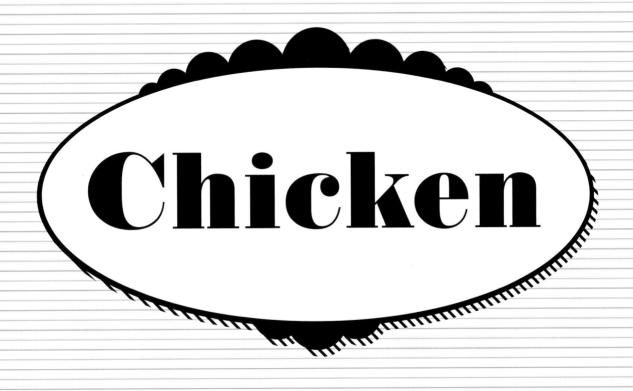

MY SOOTHING CHICKEN AND NOODLE SOUP

Chicken soup in its many guises is a cure on every continent; it has been the comforter at bedsides through the ages all over the world. Each nation makes it with a unique style. I like to make fresh pasta to boil into the soup and the kids adore helping me with the pasta machine (see the recipe opposite).

TO SERVE SIX TOTS OR FOUR GROWN-UPS

For the broth
1.5kg/3lb 5oz whole chicken *cut into four pieces*
2 carrots *peeled*
1 small onion *peeled and cut in half*
1 leek *cleaned, trimmed and cut in half*
2 ribs of celery *cleaned, trimmed and cut in half*
1 small bunch of fresh flat-leaf parsley

For the soup
2 carrots *peeled and chopped*
2 ribs of celery *cleaned, trimmed and chopped*
100g/3½oz fresh pasta or vermicelli
1 handful of chopped fresh flat-leaf parsley
a little sea salt

Use a large pan with a lid. Put all the ingredients for the broth into the pan, cover with water and set the pan on a low heat to simmer gently for 1 hour or until the chicken is cooked through.

Remove the chicken pieces and set aside on a plate. Discard the vegetables and parsley. Strain the broth into a bowl and give the pan a quick wash. Put the broth back into the pan and bring to a gentle boil, then plop in the chopped vegetables for the soup and boil until tender.

Meanwhile, discard the skin and bones from half the chicken and chop into smallish pieces (keep the rest of the chicken for sandwiches, salads or chicken pie).

Season the broth with a little salt, add the fresh pasta or vermicelli, the chicken pieces and chopped parsley and cook until the pasta is done. Serve with love.

FRESH PASTA — MAKES 500g / 1lb 2oz
(YOU WILL NEED A PASTA MACHINE!)

350g/12oz 00 flour or plain flour *plus extra to dust*
3 eggs

1 pinch of salt
butter *to serve*

Put all the ingredients for the pasta into a food processor and blitz for a couple of minutes. Scoop out and form into a ball. It should be a soft dough, so add more flour if it is wet, or a little water if it is too dry.

Dust a work surface with flour and knead the pasta well. To knead, push once with the heels of your hands away from the body, rotate the dough 90 degrees and fold it in half towards you, push once with your palms, rotate 90 degrees and fold in half towards you, push with your palms, rotate, fold, push, rotate, fold, push – continue for 10 minutes. Cover with cling film and leave to rest for 20 minutes at room temperature.

Divide the pasta into four balls. Keep three covered in cling film and divide the fourth into three equal lozenge shapes. Set the pasta machine on the highest setting and roll a lozenge through the smooth rollers into a wide sheet. Reduce the setting and roll again until it has been through all the settings, ending on the finest. Let the pasta sheets dry flat while you work all the other little balls into sheets. Each sheet should dry for about 10 minutes before running it through the tagliatelle setting.

Separate the strands of tagliatelle, making sure they do not stick together, then leave them to dry over the back of a chair. Continue until the pasta is dangling all over the house. Let it dry for 1 hour. Cook in plenty of salted boiling water, then drain and toss with butter and your favourite sauce.

CREAM OF CHICKEN SOUP WITH TARRAGON

An elegant, velvety soup that has been an English favourite at state banquets and sophisticated dinner parties for centuries.

TO SERVE FOUR TO SIX

For the broth
1 whole chicken *about 1.3kg/3lb*
1 carrot *peeled*
1 rib of celery *cleaned and trimmed*
1 onion *peeled*
1 sprig of fresh tarragon
1 leek *cleaned, trimmed and cut in half*
1 bay leaf
200ml/7fl oz white wine

For the soup
50g/2oz butter
50g/2oz plain flour
150ml/5fl oz best double cream
1 handful of chopped fresh tarragon
sea salt and freshly ground black pepper

Put all the ingredients for the broth in a pan and almost bring to the boil. Reduce the heat and gently bubble for 1½ hours until the chicken is tender. Turn off the heat and allow to cool slightly, then pop the chicken on a plate to cool, strain the stock and discard the vegetables. Return the stock to the heat and cook at a rolling boil for 20–30 minutes or until the stock has a good flavour. Strain well.

In another large pan, melt the butter and stir in the flour. Continue stirring as it bubbles for a couple of minutes, without browning, and then pour in half the stock. Stir well until you have a thickish sauce and then add the rest of the stock and boil for 20 minutes, stirring frequently.

Meanwhile, remove the skin and bones from one of the chicken breasts and cut into little chunks (keep the rest of the chicken for sandwiches, salads or chicken pie). Add to the pan with the cream and tarragon. Season to taste, heat through and serve immediately with white toast and fine butter.

MEXICAN CHICKEN SOUP
CALDO DE POLLO

A gorgeous, fragrant chicken soup with wonderful smoky Mexican flavours.

TO SERVE FOUR TO SIX

4 chicken thighs *about 500g/1lb 2oz, bone in, cut in half*
2 tsp dried oregano *(Mexican if you can find it)*
2 tbsp olive oil
2 red onions *peeled and finely chopped*
1 tsp epazote *(a Mexican herb, optional)*
1 tsp ground cinnamon
4 fat cloves of garlic *peeled and chopped*
1 tsp ground cumin

1 dried ancho chilli *seeded and stalk removed, soaked in boiling water for 20 minutes*
400g tin of re-fried beans
250ml/9fl oz good chicken or beef stock *(see pages 185 and 184)*
100ml/3½fl oz soured cream
1 handful of chopped fresh coriander
sea salt and freshly ground black pepper

Rub the chicken pieces with salt, pepper and oregano. Heat the oil in a large pan and fry the chicken until nicely browned all over. Add the onions to the pan and fry for 10 minutes, stirring every now and then. Stir in the epazote, if using, cinnamon, garlic and cumin. Strain the chilli, reserving the soaking liquid, chop it and add to the pan. Cook for a further 10 minutes, stirring occasionally.

Dollop in the re-fried beans and mix in the stock, a little at a time, until the beans are incorporated. Pour in the rest of the stock and the soaking liquid from the chilli. Season with salt and pepper and give it a good stir. Leave to tremble gently on the stove for 40 minutes.

Remove the chicken pieces and leave to cool a little, then remove the bones and skin. Chop the meat and return it to the pan, discarding the skin and bones.

Serve with a dollop of cream on top and a sprinkling of coriander and lime wedges.

MUM'S CHICKEN SOUP

This is the soup my gorgeous mum used to make for us when we were ill in bed.
I have found out it is called Avgolemono and is a very well-known Greek soup that has
been around for thousands of years. This is a very pure version. You can also add chopped,
cooked chicken meat and a little chopped dill.

TO SERVE FOUR

1 litre/1¾ pints chicken broth (*see page 184*)
2 handfuls of long grain rice or pearl barley
3 egg yolks

juice of 2 lemons
pinch of salt

Heat the broth, rice and some salt in a large pan and bring to the boil. Simmer for 20 minutes
or until the rice is cooked. Meanwhile, whisk together the egg yolks and lemon juice and ladle
a little of the broth into the mixture.

Reduce the heat and slowly pour the egg and lemon into the pan, stirring continuously.
Heat through and serve.

(JEWISH PENICILLIN) SOOTHING MATZO BALL SOUP

Traditionally, this soup is eaten during Passover, which is celebrated on the 14th day of the first month of the Jewish year, roughly the same time as Lent and Ramadan. As well as being eaten at Passover, matzo ball soup is known as an aid for invalids. It is pronounced 'mot-sa'.

TO SERVE FOUR

1 litre/1¾ pints hot chicken stock *(see page 185)*
a few flat-leaf fresh parsley leaves
a little grated lemon zest

For the matzo balls
1 egg *whisked*
2 tbsp warm chicken stock

1 heaped tsp chicken fat from the top of the stock ,or butter
1 pinch of salt
1 grind of black pepper
1 tbsp ground almonds
2 tbsp matzo meal

Mix all the ingredients for the matzo balls together and leave to stand for 1 hour.

Pour the broth and 500ml/18fl oz water into a pan with a lid and bring to the boil.

Form the matzo into balls the size of large marbles, by rolling them between your palms, drop into the soup and pop the lid on the pan. Leave to simmer for 40 minutes, then serve in bowls with the parsley and lemon zest on top.

Ching-he Huang's
HOT AND SOUR CHICKEN AND EXOTIC MUSHROOM SOUP

Ching's got great taste and is a real dynamo. Once you've prepared all the ingredients, this is a doddle to make. If you would like a thicker consistency double the quantity of cornflour. For a twist add a beaten egg when the soup boils and let it create a web-like pattern. Delicious!

TO SERVE FOUR

1 tbsp groundnut oil
350g/12oz skinless chicken breast fillets
2.5cm/1 inch piece of fresh root ginger *peeled and grated*
1 clove of garlic *peeled and crushed*
1 red chilli *finely chopped*
100g/3½oz shredded Chinese leaf
150g/5oz exotic mushrooms
such as torn oyster, sliced shiitake, enoki
150g/5oz chestnut mushrooms *sliced*

200g tin bamboo shoots *drained and finely sliced*
750ml/1¼ pints hot vegetable stock
2 tbsp Chinese cooking wine or dry sherry
2 tbsp light soy sauce
1 tbsp rice vinegar
3 tbsp cornflour mixed with 4tbsp cold water
1 spring onion *trimmed and sliced*
1 small handful of roughly chopped fresh coriander
lime wedges *to serve*

Heat a large wok or pan over a high heat and add the groundnut oil. Add the chicken and stir-fry for 4–5 minutes until pale golden.

Add the ginger, garlic and chilli and stir-fry for a few seconds. Add the Chinese leaf and all the mushrooms and stir-fry for 1 minute. Add the bamboo shoots, hot stock, wine or sherry, soy, vinegar and blended cornflour. Bring to the boil and simmer for a further minute.

Remove from the heat, garnish with spring onion and coriander and serve immediately with wedges of lime.

COQ AU VIN

This classic French dish is as warm and comforting as a bright autumn day. If you can get your mitts on some fresh wild mushrooms, so much the better – chanterelle, morel, cep or field mushrooms would all be delicious. I have used handfuls of dried ceps and morels because they add a lovely extra flavour. As with most stews, this is best eaten a couple of days after it is made.

TO SERVE EIGHT TO TEN

2 tbsp olive oil
100g/3½ oz butter
200g/7oz bacon lardons
1 handful each dried cep and morel mushrooms *soaked in boiling water for 20 minutes (optional)*
2 small corn-fed chickens *each cut into ten pieces*
300g/11oz baby button mushrooms *trimmed and quartered*
1 large handful of chopped fresh flat-leaf parsley

3 fat cloves of garlic *peeled*
2 heaped tbsp plain flour
1 tbsp cognac or brandy
1 bottle of hefty red wine *such as Cabernet Sauvignon*
500ml/18fl oz good chicken stock *(see page 185)*
1 bouquet garni of fresh thyme and 3 bay leaves
500g/1lb 2oz pearl onions *peeled*
sea salt and freshly ground black pepper

Preheat the oven to 150ºC/300ºF/gas mark 2. Heat the oil in a large pan with a lid and fry the lardons until they begin to brown.

Strain the dried mushrooms, if using, reserving the soaking liquid. Chop them and add to the pan with the chicken pieces. Season with pepper and fry until the skin of the chicken is browned all over. Remove the lardons and chicken mixture and set aside on a plate.

Reduce the heat and fry the button mushrooms in the remaining oil in the pan, and throw in the parsley, half the butter and garlic. Stir through and gently fry for a couple of minutes.

cont.

cont.

Stir in the flour until it absorbs the fat, then pour in the soaking liquid from the mushrooms, the cognac or brandy and a little of the red wine. Stir into a smooth paste, gradually add more wine and continue stirring until all the wine is incorporated. Pour in the stock. Pop in the bouquet garni and simmer for a few minutes, then return the chicken and lardons to the pan and season to taste. Cover with the lid and pop in the oven for 1 hour.

Meanwhile, boil the onions in lightly salted water for 10 minutes, strain, reserving the liquid, and then gently fry in the remaining butter until golden.

Add them to the chicken when the pan comes out of the oven. You can use the liquid that the onions were boiled in to add to the pan if it needs more juice. Check the seasoning and serve with mashed potatoes (see page 187) and buttered Savoy cabbage.

Caroline Conran's
CHICKEN AND MUSHROOM STEW

This is one of my wonderful mum's excellent stews. She has based it on a traditional Catalan recipe that uses veal scallopine. This scrumptious dish takes about half the time to cook than the veal version, but is equally sublime.

TO SERVE FOUR TO SIX

1 onion *peeled and finely chopped*
4–5 tbsp olive oil
1 tomato *peeled and chopped (see page 121)*
3–4 tbsp flour
750g/1lb 11oz skinless chicken breast fillets
sliced into escalopes

750g/1lb 11oz mixed fresh mushrooms
button, chestnut, Portobello, and shiitake or any wild mushrooms, cut into thick slices
250ml/9fl oz dry white wine
250ml/9fl oz good chicken stock *(see page 185)*
sea salt and freshly ground black pepper

Soften the onion in 3 tablespoons of the oil in a small pan, stirring occasionally. When it turns golden, add the tomatoes and stir; keep the heat fairly hot while they become jammy, but take care they do not burn.

Shake the flour over the chicken escalopes and season them with salt and pepper. Heat a little oil in a casserole that is going to be large enough to hold all the mushrooms. Fry the escalopes quickly on each side a few at a time, removing them as they turn golden.

When they are all fried, return them to the casserole adding the mushrooms. Sprinkle with the remaining flour, stir through and add the white wine. Simmer for 5 minutes, then add the stock. Lastly, add the tomatoes and onions and season with salt and pepper. Cover, then bring to the boil and simmer gently for 20–25 minutes, until the chicken is cooked and tender.

FRAGRANT CHICKEN STEW

Full of wonderful aromatic ingredients which make a homely and lip-smacking dinner.

TO SERVE SIX

1 tbsp olive oil
1 large chicken *cut into eight pieces*
1 walnut-sized knob of butter
3 small red onions *peeled and chopped*
2 cloves of garlic *peeled and chopped*
1 walnut-sized piece of fresh root ginger *peeled and chopped*
1 tsp ground cumin

1 butternut squash *peeled, seeded and chopped into 3cm/1¼ inch cubes*
4 large tomatoes *each cut into eight pieces*
1 pinch of saffron threads
500ml/18fl oz good chicken stock *(see page 185)*
2 strips of lemon zest *(use a potato peeler)*
1 handful of chopped fresh flat-leaf parsley
sea salt and freshly ground black pepper

Preheat the oven to 220°C/425°F/gas mark 7. Heat the oil in an ovenproof pot with a lid, on a medium to high heat, and brown the chicken pieces on both sides. Remove the chicken from the pot and put them aside on a plate until needed.

Reduce the heat, add the butter to the pot and gently fry the onions, stirring from time to time, until soft – about 10 minutes.

Stir in the garlic, ginger and cumin and cook for 2 minutes, then add the squash to the pot and gently fry for 5 minutes, making sure it does not burn. Stir in the tomatoes, saffron and stock and bring to a gentle simmer, then remove the pot from the heat.

Submerge the chicken pieces and lemon zest in the vegetables, then season well with salt and pepper. Give it a final stir through, put on the lid and pop it in the oven for 1 hour. Take out of the oven, season to taste and stir in the chopped parsley.

This is lovely served with rosemary roast new potatoes (see page 188) and cooked spinach that's been tossed in warm butter and nutmeg.

CHICKEN, CHORIZO AND BUTTERBEAN STEW

If you prefer, you can use chicken pieces with bones in: brown them as for the breasts and return them to this mouthwatering stew when you add the passata.

TO SERVE EIGHT TO TEN

2 tbsp olive oil
8 boneless, skinless chicken breasts *seasoned with salt and pepper*
1 Spanish chorizo (about 250g/9oz) *skinned and sliced*
4 carrots *peeled and chopped*
2 onions *peeled and chopped*
2 ribs of celery *cleaned, trimmed and chopped*

7 cloves of garlic *peeled and chopped*
1 tsp finely chopped fresh thyme
50g/2oz butter
500g/1lb 2oz tomato passata
2 x 400g tins of chopped tomatoes
2 x 400g tins of butter beans *drained*
1 large handful of chopped fresh flat-leaf parsley
sea salt and freshly ground black pepper

Heat the oil in a large pot and plop in 4 of the chicken breasts. Brown them on both sides (they should remain slightly raw in the middle) and then put them aside on a plate. Repeat with the rest of the chicken pieces.

Fry the chorizo chunks in the pot until they begin to crisp. Dump in the carrots, onions, celery, garlic, thyme and butter and stew for about 20 minutes, stirring frequently and breaking up the chorizo pieces with a spoon. Once the vegetables are nice and soft, stir the passata, tomatoes and beans into the pot and leave to bubble for a further hour, stirring from time to time.

Cut the chicken into nice juicy chunks, about 5cm x 5cm/2 inches x 2 inches, and throw into the pot. Cook for a further 15 minutes until the chicken is cooked through but still tender. Stir through the parsley, season to taste and serve with roast potatoes.

CARIBBEAN COCONUT CURRY

This gorgeous one-pot curry is very hot and spicy, so if you want a milder flavour, don't use as many Scotch bonnets. I have chopped them in a blender to avoid any mishaps from touching them, as they are some of the hottest chillies on the planet and burn like hell.

TO SERVE SIX

3 tbsp olive oil
6 large chicken thighs *or 1 chicken cut into six pieces*
50g/2oz butter
2 large onions *peeled and sliced*
1 tbsp peeled and chopped fresh root ginger
6 fat cloves of garlic *peeled and chopped*
1–3 Scotch bonnet chillies *stalks removed*
2 tsp freshly ground black pepper
1 tsp each ground turmeric and allspice

2 tsp each ground cumin, coriander seeds and cinnamon
400ml/14fl oz coconut milk
600ml/1 pint chicken stock *(see page 185)*
600g/1lb 5oz sweet potato *peeled and cut into 3cm/1¼ inch cubes*
400g tin of red kidney beans *drained*
6 handfuls of basmati rice
sea salt

Heat 2 tablespoons of the olive oil in a large pot. Season the chicken pieces and brown them on both sides in the pot, then remove and keep aside until needed. Reduce the heat and drop the butter and onions into the pot and gently stew for 20 minutes, stirring occasionally.

Pulse the ginger, garlic, chillies and pepper in a blender until finely chopped. Stir the mixture into the onions and continue frying for 5 minutes. Pour the rest of the olive oil into the pot, then add the cumin, coriander and cinnamon and stir-fry for another 5 minutes.

Pour in a little of the coconut milk and scrape the bottom of the pan so all the tasty bits that are stuck to the bottom amalgamate into the sauce. Add the rest of the coconut milk, the stock, sweet potato and salt to taste and return the chicken to the pan. Stir through and gently simmer for 30 minutes. Stir in the beans and rice and continue simmering for another 30 minutes, or until the rice is cooked. Season to taste.

LEMON CHICKEN WITH SPINACH

A fresh and healthy dish, bursting with gorgeous flavours.

TO SERVE EIGHT

2 tbsp olive oil
8 fat or 16 small chicken thighs
50g/2oz butter
2 onions *peeled and sliced*
½ tsp ground turmeric
1 tsp each ground cinnamon, cumin
and coriander
1 walnut-sized piece of fresh root ginger
peeled and chopped

3 fat cloves of garlic *peeled and chopped*
250g/9oz baby new potatoes *cut in half*
400g tin of chickpeas *drained*
500ml/18fl oz good chicken stock *(see page 185)*
400g/14oz young spinach *washed*
grated zest of 1 lemon
sea salt and freshly ground black pepper
plain yoghurt *to serve*

Heat the oil on a medium to high heat in a large pan with a lid. Season the chicken pieces with salt and pepper and brown on both sides. Remove from the pan and set aside.

Reduce the heat, dump the butter and onions into the pan and sauté for 15 minutes, stirring frequently. Sprinkle in all the spices, the ginger, garlic, some salt and a really good grind of pepper. Stir through and gently fry for a further 5 minutes.

Add the potatoes, chickpeas and stock and return the chicken to the pan. Leave to simmer for 45 minutes.

Stir in half the spinach and the lemon zest and cook down for 5 minutes. Add the rest of the spinach and cook for a further 20 minutes. Season to taste and serve with basmati rice and a dollop of yoghurt.

CHICKEN CURRY FOR LITTLE CHICKENS

This is a really simple storecupboard staple. My kids love it and have had it hundreds of times. It always varies slightly. Sometimes I put cubes of butternut squash in, or cooked French beans. Have a play to find your favourite.

SERVES EIGHT LITTLE CHICKENS OR FOUR OLD HENS

4 boneless, skinless chicken breasts
2 tbsp olive oil
2 red onions *peeled and chopped*
50g/2oz butter
1 walnut-sized piece of fresh root ginger *peeled and chopped*

1 tsp garam masala
400g tin of chopped plum tomatoes
½ tsp sugar
100ml/3½fl oz double cream or yoghurt
sea salt and freshly ground black pepper

Season the chicken breasts with a tiny bit of salt and pepper and then fry them in the oil in a large pan for 3–5 minutes on each side or until browned on the outside but still a little pink in the middle. Remove from the pan and set aside.

Reduce the heat, then dump the onions and butter into the pan and sauté for 15 minutes, or until soft. Stir in the ginger and garam masala and fry for a further 5 minutes, then pour in the tomatoes. Stir through and leave to stew for 20 minutes, stirring every now and then.

Cut the chicken into bite-sized pieces, return to the pan and stir in the sugar, cream or yoghurt and 100ml/3½fl oz of water. Bring to a gentle bubble for 5 minutes. Season to taste and serve with basmati rice, French beans or broccoli.

SLOPPY, SPICY, RED CHICKEN STEW

This is a wonderful winter stew, rich and luxurious. It's at its greatest when eaten by candlelight on a long, cold winter night.

TO SERVE FOUR TO SIX

1 chicken (about 1kg/2¼lb) *cut into pieces*
1 dried chilli *crushed*
1 tsp each ground coriander and paprika
2 tbsp olive oil
2 red onions *peeled and sliced*
50g/2oz butter
2 red peppers *cored, seeded and cut into strips*

150g/5oz Spanish chorizo *skinned and cut into 1cm/½ inch cubes*
150ml/5fl oz red wine
1 pinch of saffron threads
4 tomatoes *peeled, seeded and quartered (see Tip)*
sea salt and freshly ground black pepper

Pile the chicken into a large bowl and sprinkle over the chilli, coriander and paprika. Season with salt and pepper and mix to coat all the chicken pieces with the spices.

Heat the oil in a large pan and fry the chicken until browned all over. Remove from the pan and set aside.

Reduce the heat, then dump the onions, butter, red peppers and chorizo into the pan and fry for 20 minutes, stirring every now and then, until you have a lovely soft mass of relaxed veg. Glug in the wine, crush the saffron between your fingers and stir it into the pan along with the chicken pieces and the tomatoes. Season with salt and pepper and simmer for 1 hour, giving it a loving poke and a stir every now and again. Serve with rosemary roast potatoes (see page 188) and buttered runner beans.

TIP To peel tomatoes, bring a large pan of water to the boil, then remove from the heat. Drop the tomatoes in and leave to stand for 2–3 minutes or until the skins split when poked with a sharp knife. Remove to a large bowl to cool. When cool enough, slip off the skins.

FISH SOUPS

Skye Gyngell's
LOBSTER BONNE FEMME

OYSTER AND WATERCRESS SOUP

LANGOUSTINE AND CLAM BURRIDA

Terence Conran's
BISQUE

SPICY THAI BROTH WITH PRAWNS AND LANGOUSTINE

Mark Hix's
VICHYSSOISE WITH OYSTERS

CORN CHOWDER

CORN BREAD

FISH STEWS

BOUILLABAISSE WITH ROUILLE AND CROUTONS

GOAN PRAWN CURRY

GAMBAS PIL-PIL

JAMBALAYA

INKY SQUID STEW

CREOLE PRAWN AND CHICKEN GUMBO

MOULES MARINIÈRES

Skye Gyngell's

LOBSTER BONNE FEMME

Skye's cooking is exceptional and innovative, and always irresistible. In this recipe, plump, sweet lobster meat is warmed through in a sauce with leeks, potato pieces and thyme.

TO SERVE FOUR

2 live medium lobsters
500g/1lb 2oz peeled potatoes *(Desiree are good)* *cut into irregular bite-sized chunks*
4 tbsp unsalted butter
200g/7oz small young leeks *cleaned, trimmed and left whole*
1 splash of vermouth

a few sprigs of fresh thyme *(lemon thyme imparts a particularly lovely flavour into soups and stews)*
350ml/12fl oz chicken stock *(see page 185)*
75g/3oz shelled cooked fresh peas
1 tbsp finely chopped fresh flat-leaf parsley
sea salt

Place a large pot of salty water on to boil. When the water is vigorously boiling, drop in the lobsters and cook them for around 8 minutes. Remove them from the water. When they are cool enough to handle, take a sharp knife and make an incision all the way down the middle. Take out the flesh, then crack the claws and gently remove the meat from them, too.

Place the potatoes in a saucepan, add enough cold water to cover and set over a medium heat. Season with salt. Cook them at a gentle simmer until tender when pierced with a fork. Drain them and set aside. Melt 1 tbsp of the butter in a deep-sided skillet over a gentle heat.

When the butter has melted, add the leeks, vermouth, thyme, and, finally, chicken stock. Allow the broth to come to a simmer. Add the remaining butter and swirl until it melts. Taste for salt. Turn the heat down to low and add the potatoes, lobster pieces and peas. Swirl and tilt the pan to baste the lobster in the buttery broth.

Cook for a further 4 minutes or so to allow the sauce's flavour to slightly intensify and reduce, and to ensure that the lobster is completely warmed through. Ladle into bowls and serve immediately with a simple green salad and a crunchy textural bread.

OYSTER AND WATERCRESS SOUP

Woody Allen once said, 'I will not eat oysters. I want my food dead. Not sick, not wounded, dead.' Well, in this recipe the oysters are actually cooked for several minutes, so at least you know for certain that they won't jump off the plate. This soup is really rather easy to make, but makes a very elegant treat. It is also great with spinach.

TO SERVE FOUR

12 live oysters in the shell
150ml/5fl oz white wine
500ml/18fl oz chicken stock *(see page 185)*
50g/2oz butter
1 shallot *peeled and finely chopped*
1 rib of celery *cleaned, trimmed and finely chopped*
1 clove of garlic *peeled and finely chopped*

1 heaped tbsp plain flour
50g/2oz basmati rice
½ tsp grated nutmeg
2 tsp Worcestershire sauce
300ml/10fl oz single cream
4 handfuls of fresh watercress *washed and chopped*
sea salt and freshly ground black pepper

Shuck the oysters over a bowl, strain the juice and pour it into a large pan. Add the wine and stock and bring to the boil. Reduce the heat, add the oysters and poach for 4 minutes. Remove the oysters and put to one side, and reserve the juice in a heatproof bowl.

Melt the butter in the pan and sauté the shallot for 10 minutes without browning. Add the celery and garlic and fry for 4 minutes. Add the flour and cook for a couple of minutes, stirring continuously. Slowly add the oyster juice, whisking with a spoon, and bring to the boil. Add the rice and reduce the heat slightly, then add the nutmeg and Worcestershire sauce and simmer for 10 minutes.

Add the cream, stir in the watercress and cook for 4 minutes. Season to taste, add the oysters, heat through and serve.

LANGOUSTINE AND CLAM BURRIDA

Burrida is a sensational Italian fish stew, with all the flavours of the sea, enhanced by pine nuts, herbs and wine. There are many variations of this dish; some add tomatoes, others use walnuts instead of pine nuts. Skate is often used, as is dogfish (with its liver mashed into the sauce). Ask your fishmonger to clean and prepare the squid for you or see the Tip on page 144 if you want to have a go yourself.

TO SERVE FOUR

2 tbsp olive oil
50g/2oz butter
1 carrot *peeled and finely sliced*
1 rib of celery *cleaned, trimmed and finely sliced*
1 onion *peeled and finely sliced*
1 handful of pine nuts
3 anchovy fillets *chopped*
3 cloves of garlic *peeled and roughly chopped*
150ml/5fl oz white wine
500ml/18fl oz fish stock *(see page 185)*

2 raw squid *cleaned and sliced*
300g/11oz hake or monkfish *skinned, boned and cut into 2cm/¾ inch cubes*
4 raw langoustine *washed*
300g/11oz raw clams in their shells *washed*
1 large handful of chopped fresh basil
4 slices of baguette, *either toasted or fried, and rubbed with 1 peeled clove of garlic*
1 lemon *cut into eight pieces*

Heat the oil and butter in a large pan with a lid, over a medium heat. Plop in the carrot, celery and onion and gently fry, without browning, for 10 minutes, stirring often.

Meanwhile, mash the pine nuts, anchovies and garlic together in a pestle and mortar or blender. Stir into the pan and fry for a couple of minutes, then pour in the wine. Simmer for 5 minutes, then stir in the stock and squid and leave to simmer for 30 minutes.

Drop in the hake or monkfish, langoustine, clams and basil, pop on the lid and cook for just under 10 minutes or until the langoustine are pink, the clams are open, and the chunks of fish are just cooked through. Discard any clams that don't open. Break up the garlic bread into pieces and divide between the bowls. Ladle the soup over and serve with a langoustine each and slices of lemon. I would advise the use of large napkins and bowls to clatter the used shells into. Enjoy.

Terence Conran's
BISQUE

Being a war baby, my fabulous dad is always happiest when using up leftovers and this soup has to be his all-time favourite. The leftover lobster, prawn, crayfish or crab shells and any meaty bits are used to make a luxurious soup.

TO SERVE FOUR TO SIX

2 lobster or crab shells *or as many prawn or crayfish shells as will fit in the pot, together with the remaining leg, claw and body parts*
75ml/3fl oz brandy or Armagnac
1 onion *peeled and roughly chopped*
1 carrot *peeled and roughly chopped*
1 rib of celery *cleaned, trimmed and chopped*
1 tbsp tomato purée

150ml/5fl oz white wine
1–2 dashes of anchovy essence
1 bouquet garni
sea salt and freshly ground black pepper

To serve
cayenne pepper
Jersey cream *(optional)*

Preheat the oven to 200°C/400°F/gas mark 6. Put the shells and other bits and pieces together in a roasting tin and place them in the oven for about 15 minutes until they are slightly charred.

Take the tin out of the oven, pour the brandy or Armagnac over the shells and ignite. When the flames have died down, tip the lot into a flameproof casserole with the onion, carrot, celery, tomato purée, wine, anchovy essence, bouquet garni and enough water to cover. Bring to the boil and simmer for 2 hours.

Remove the larger pieces of shell, and then blend the liquid in a strong blender. Strain through a conical sieve. Depending on how gravelly you like your bisque, add a spoonful or two of the sludgy shell left in the sieve. Adjust the seasoning and add a dash or two more of anchovy essence.

Serve very hot with a sprinkling of cayenne pepper. For a luxurious velvety touch, you can add a spoonful or two of cream.

SPICY THAI BROTH WITH PRAWNS AND LANGOUSTINE

A beautiful clean soup that can vary in heat depending on the type of chillies you use, and whether the seeds are left in or not. I have removed them for a little less heat. It is one of the prettiest soups I know.

TO SERVE FOUR

For the prawn broth
1 carrot, *peeled*
1 rib of celery *cleaned and trimmed*
1 tomato
6 lime leaves
1 chilli *cut in half lengthways and seeded*
1 bunch of fresh coriander
1 small onion *peeled*
2 sticks of lemon grass

8 large raw prawns and 4 raw langoustine
with their shells and heads
sea salt to taste

For the soup
2 tbsp sherry
1 tbsp Thai fish sauce
1 chilli *cut in half lengthways, seeded and cut into very thin strips*
12 fresh coriander leaves

Put all the ingredients for the broth except the prawns, langoustine and salt into a large pot and cover with 1.5 litres/2½ pints of water. Bring to the boil, reduce the heat and tremble for 10 minutes. Salt the broth and drop in the prawns and langoustine. Simmer for another 5 minutes, remove the prawns and langoustine and set aside to cool. Leave the broth on the heat for another 40 minutes.

Meanwhile, peel and de-vein the shellfish, throwing the heads and shells back into the broth pot as you go. Strain the broth through a muslin-lined sieve and discard the vegetable shells then clean the pan. Return the broth to the pan. Stir in the sherry, fish sauce, prawns and langoustine and heat through.

Serve in wide bowls with 3 or 4 strips of chilli, a few coriander leaves, 2 prawns and 1 langoustine on top of each.

Mark Hix's
VICHYSSOISE WITH OYSTERS

Mark is one of the brightest jewels in London's culinary crown. Since this chilled soup was invented by a French chef at the Algonquin Hotel in New York in 1917, many people have developed their own version. The most important thing is to get maximum flavour from the potatoes. Avoid waxy potatoes – Mark recommends Roseval or Maris Piper. Don't cook the hell out of them either; they need to be cooked just until soft, then cooled quickly to preserve the flavour. The addition of the oysters gives it an indulgent feel. If you want to take this further, why not try a spoonful of caviar on top?

TO SERVE FOUR

1 tbsp olive oil
2 medium leeks *cleaned, trimmed, roughly chopped*
250g/9oz well-flavoured new or old potatoes *(see above)* peeled and roughly chopped
1 litre/1¾ pints vegetable stock *(or Marigold bouillon powder or a good-quality vegetable stock cube dissolved in that amount of hot water)*
2–3 spring onions *trimmed and roughly chopped*

8 oysters *removed from their shell and juices reserved*
salt and freshly ground black pepper

For the garnish
1 small waxy potato *cut into 1cm/½ inch dice and cooked until tender in boiling salted water*
½ small leek *cleaned, trimmed, cut into 1cm/½ inch dice and cooked until just tender in boiling salted water*
1 tbsp finely chopped fresh chives

Heat the oil in a pan with a lid, add the leeks, cover the pan and cook without allowing them to colour for 4–5 minutes. Add the potatoes and stock, bring to the boil and lightly season with salt and pepper. Simmer for 10–15 minutes, or until the potatoes are just tender. Add the spring onions and 4 of the oysters with their juices and simmer for another 2 minutes.

Blend until smooth in a liquidiser, then strain through a fine-meshed sieve. Adjust the seasoning, if necessary. Allow the soup to cool down in a bowl over some iced or cold water, stirring occasionally. When the soup is cold it will thicken, so you may need to adjust the consistency with a little more stock or milk as you prefer. Add the potato and leek garnish and stir in well. Serve in shallow soup/pasta bowls with one of the reserved oysters in each bowl, sprinkled with the chives.

TIP Use any mollusc in place of the oysters.

CORN CHOWDER

Chowder must be the all-American, all-time favourite and, like all the classics, it can be made in myriad variations. It originated in mid-18th century France and its name probably comes from the French term 'chaudière' or 'stew pot'. A famous type of American chowder is New England Clam Chowder. It is such a well-known dish, made with potatoes, onion, pork and clams, that a bill was raised in Maine in the 1930s making the use of tomatoes in Clam Chowder a criminal offence. This is a delicious chowder recipes, without tomatoes, and once you get the hang of it you can start to improvise, adding your own wonderful ingredients.

TO SERVE EIGHT

2 tbsp olive oil
150g/5oz bacon lardons
200g/7oz new potatoes *cut into quarters*
50g/2oz butter
1 onion *peeled and chopped*
1 tbsp plain flour
1 litre/1¾ pints milk

8 splashes of Tabasco
300g/11oz skinless, boneless, sustainable cod *cut into 1cm/½ inch cubes*
340g tin of sweetcorn kernels
25g/1oz chopped fresh chives or chopped fresh flat-leaf parsley
sea salt and freshly ground black pepper
corn bread *(see overleaf) to serve*

Put a large pot on a medium heat, glug in a little oil and fry the lardons until crisp. Dump in the potatoes, butter and onion and stir through for about 5 minutes or until soft. Sprinkle in the flour and continue stirring while you gradually add the milk until you have a smooth consistency. Season with the Tabasco, salt and pepper and leave to gently simmer for 20 minutes, or until the potatoes are just cooked.

Stirring often, drop in the fish and corn and continue cooking for a further 10 minutes, stirring often. Stir in the chives or parsley and adjust the seasoning. I like lots of black pepper. Serve with the corn bread to serve(see overleaf).

TIP 500g/1lb 2oz of fresh clams popped into the soup five minutes before the end of cooking with a lid slammed on is gorgeous, too.

CORN BREAD — MAKES ENOUGH FOR 2 X 20.5CM/8 INCH ROUND CAKE TINS

125g/4oz melted butter *plus a little extra to grease*
250g/9oz plain flour
200g/7oz polenta or semolina
1 tbsp salt
3 tsp baking powder
2 tsp bicarbonate of soda

1 tbsp raw cane sugar
400ml/14fl oz milk
2 eggs
2 chillies *cut in half lengthways, seeded and finely chopped*
2 x 340g tins of sweetcorn kernels

Preheat the oven to 220°C/425°F/gas mark 7. Grease two 20.5cm/8 inch round cake tins and line the bottom with greaseproof paper.

Mix everything except the chillies and sweetcorn into a smooth, sloppy batter, then throw in the corn with its juice and the chillies. Mix through and pour the mixture into the cake tins. Pop in the oven for 20 minutes, or until golden and springy to the touch.

Cool slightly before slicing and then spread with butter.

BOUILLABAISSE WITH ROUILLE AND CROUTONS

Bouillabaisse, a classic rich and spicy French fish stew, originates from the port city of Marseilles. It is traditionally served with chunks of toasted bread and piquant mayonnaise. The origins of this stew date back to the Ancient Greeks when they founded Marseilles around 600BC. Their simple fish stew was called 'Kakavia', but over time it evolved into the famous bouillabaisse, which appears in Roman mythology as the dish that Venus fed to Vulcan to lull him to sleep so that she could secretly seduce Mars. Bad girl!

TO SERVE SIX

18 mussels *scrubbed and beards removed*
1 walnut-sized knob of butter
2 tbsp olive oil
2 onions *peeled and finely chopped*
2 ribs of celery white parts only, *cleaned, trimmed and chopped*
2 fennel bulbs *trimmed and cut into eighths*
2 carrots *peeled and chopped*
3 cloves of garlic *peeled and chopped*
1 leek *white parts only, cleaned and trimmed*
300ml/10fl oz white wine
1 large pinch of saffron threads
2 slices of orange peel *(use a potato peeler)*
400g tin of plum tomatoes
200g/7oz tomato passata
1.5 litres/2½ pints water or fish stock *(see page 185)*
12 new potatoes, peeled and quartered
300g/11oz hake fillet *cut into 3cm/1¼ inch cubes*

300g/11oz cod fillet *cut into 4cm/1¼ inch cubes*
300g/11oz halibut steak *cut into 3cm/1½ inch cubes*
6 langoustine
sea salt and freshly ground black pepper
200g/7oz grated Gruyère *to serve*

For the garlic croutons
1 baguette *cut into slices*
2 cloves of garlic *peeled*

For the rouille
2 egg yolks
1 pinch of saffron threads *crumbled*
1 clove of garlic *peeled and finely chopped*
½ tsp pimento powder
300ml/10fl oz olive oil
300ml/10fl oz sunflower oil
1 tbsp water

Firstly make the croutons and rouille. Toast the slices of bread until crisp and browned and rub with the garlic. Mix the egg yolks, saffron, garlic and pimento in a medium bowl.

cont.

cont.

Very slowly at first, drizzle in the oils, mixing well and stirring to make sure the oils are amalgamated into the egg yolks. The mixture should get thicker and thicker. When it becomes really thick, add the water. Continue adding the rest of the oil.

The mixing can also be done in a food processor, which makes it very quick and easy. I like to do mine by hand as it is a very satisfying process, watching the change of the bright yellow egg yolks into a thick and oily orange sauce.

Now prepare the stew. Discard any mussels that don't close when tapped. Put the butter and oil in a large casserole on a medium heat. Cook the onions, celery, fennel, carrot, garlic and leek slowly, stirring from time to time, until the onions become translucent.

Add the wine, saffron and orange zest and boil rapidly for 5 minutes. Add the tomatoes and passata, turn down the heat and simmer for a further 10 minutes. Add the water or stock and the potatoes and cook for 5 minutes. Season to taste, then add the fish and simmer for 5 minutes. Add the mussels and langoustine and simmer for a further 5 minutes. Discard any mussels that don't open.

Ladle into bowls and serve with the rouille dolloped onto the garlic croutons and sprinkled with Gruyère.

TIP If the rouille curdles or separates, try adding some ice cubes and mixing well. Remove the ice when the mixture comes together again. The other rescue remedy is to start with another egg yolk and slowly mix in the curdled rouille.

GOAN PRAWN CURRY

Goa is India's smallest state and stretches along the southwest coast of India. Because of its coastline and beautiful beaches, seafood and rice form the main part of the Goan diet. Goan curries traditionally include various nuts such as cashews and coconuts which grow in abundance in the area.

TO SERVE FOUR

For the Goan curry paste
1 chilli *stalk removed*
1 walnut-sized piece of fresh root ginger *peeled and chopped*
4 cloves of garlic *peeled and chopped*
2 tsp tamarind paste
½ tsp ground turmeric
1 tsp each ground cumin and coriander
2 tbsp olive oil

For the Goan prawn curry
2 tbsp olive oil
1 large onion *peeled and finely sliced*
1 tsp freshly ground black pepper
1kg/2¼lb large raw prawns *peeled and deveined*
200ml/7fl oz coconut milk
1 large bunch of chopped fresh coriander
sea salt

Place all the ingredients for the curry paste except the oil in a blender and blitz, then, with the machine still running, slowly drizzle in the oil. Turn out into a bowl.

To make the curry, heat the oil in a large pan and gently fry the onion and black pepper for about 10 minutes or until the onion is soft, without browning, stirring often. Add the curry paste and stir through, then turn up the heat a little and fry for 5 minutes, stirring frequently. Reduce the heat and throw the prawns into the pan. Stir continuously for another 5 minutes, then slowly pour in the coconut milk, stirring until you have a smooth sauce. Continue cooking and stirring for another 5 minutes.

Finally, stir in the coriander, season with salt to taste and serve with boiled rice. I like to have a sliced banana with a little lime squeezed over the top with this delicious curry.

GAMBAS PIL-PIL

Pil-pil is a superb and simple dish from the Spanish coast. It is best cooked in an earthenware dish and brought sizzling to the table. Traditionally, it is served at about 5pm with a cool glass of wine. Good, rustic bread is essential for mopping up the fabulous oil at the end. Remember to keep the heat low, as you do not want burnt garlic.

TO SERVE SIX AS A STARTER

100ml/3½fl oz olive oil *(Spanish would be best)*
2 cloves of garlic *peeled and very, very finely chopped*
1 red chilli *cut in half lengthways, seeded and very, very finely chopped*
1 tsp Spanish paprika

750g/1lb 11oz large raw prawns *peeled with the tails left on, and deveined (use the shells for stock)*
1 handful of chopped fresh flat-leaf parsley
sea salt and freshly ground black pepper
lemon wedges *to serve*

Heat the oil over a low heat in an earthenware dish or a frying pan. Drop in the garlic, chilli, paprika and a pinch of salt and stew for 5 minutes.

Plop in the prawns and stir about. Keep gently prodding, stirring and turning the prawns until they turn pink and curl up completely – about 10 minutes.

Scatter in the parsley and stir through. Season with pepper and bring to the table with lemon wedges and bread.

JAMBALAYA

Jambalaya is a fabulous dish from New Orleans, the cultural melting pot in the swamps of Louisiana. It appears that the parent dish is paella, brought to the region by the Spanish. Evolved and adapted by myriad cultures and the available ingredients, it mutated into what we now know as jambalaya. The swamps were alive with alligators, turtles, frogs, oysters and shrimp, and any of these meats can happily be thrown into the pot. My version uses prawns and chorizo, not as exotic, but quite delicious.

TO SERVE SIX TO EIGHT

1 tbsp plain flour
1 tsp dried oregano
2 tsp paprika
½ tsp celery seeds
750g/1lb 11oz chicken thighs *(eight pieces)*
2 tbsp olive oil
225g/8oz hard Spanish chorizo *skinned and sliced*
3 cloves of garlic *peeled and chopped*
500g/1lb 2oz raw shelled prawns
1 onion *peeled and finely sliced*

1 celery heart *leaves and all*
2 red peppers *halved lengthways, cored, seeded and cut into fine slices*
1 tsp dried thyme
5 tomatoes *peeled, seeded and cut into quarters (see page 121)*
6 handfuls of long-grain rice
1–4 tbsp Tabasco sauce
1 handful of chopped fresh flat-leaf parsley
sea salt and freshly ground black pepper

Mix the flour, oregano, half the paprika, the celery seeds and some salt and pepper in a large bowl. Drop in the chicken thighs and turn with your hands to coat in the flour and spices. Heat the oil in a large pan big enough to take the chicken in one layer, and brown the chicken pieces until golden on both sides. Return them to the bowl with the flour.

Fry the chorizo in the oil for a few minutes, then reduce the heat and stir in the rest of the paprika, a little salt, the garlic and prawns. Stir until the prawns turn pink, then add the onion, celery, red peppers and thyme to the pan. Continue stirring every now and then until the onion is soft – about 10 minutes. Return the chicken and any remaining flour to the pan, stir in the tomatoes, sprinkle in the rice and cover with water. Give it a good stir, then bring to a gentle boil and simmer until the rice is cooked – stirring occasionally – about 40 minutes. Season to taste with salt, pepper and Tabasco and stir through the parsley.

INKY SQUID STEW

This magnificent stew looks like a real witches' brew. It is a fantastic colour and the squid is wonderfully tender. Do not eat it on a first date though as it makes your teeth black! You should be able to get hold of sachets of squid ink at some fishmongers, or online. It also comes in useful if your pen runs out of ink.

TO SERVE FOUR TO SIX

50g/2oz butter
2 tbsp olive oil
2 large red onions *peeled and chopped*
1kg/2¼lb squid *cleaned and cut into 1cm/½ inch strips (see Tip)*
4 cloves of garlic *peeled and chopped*
⅓ bottle of heavy-duty red wine *such as Merlot or Shiraz*

400g tin of plum tomatoes
3 sachets of squid or cuttlefish ink
½ tube tomato purée
1 tbsp Dijon mustard
10 dashes of Tabasco sauce
1 tbsp redcurrant jelly
1 tsp herbes de Provence
sea salt and freshly ground black pepper

Heat the butter and oil in a large casserole. Dump in the onions and gently fry for about 10 minutes, stirring them about to make sure they don't brown but become soft and sweet. Dump the squid into the pot, turn up the heat and stir until the squid has changed from translucent to opaque. Reduce the heat, stir in the garlic and fry for 1 minute, then stir in the rest of the ingredients. Gently bubble your witches' brew for 2 hours, stirring occasionally.

Add a little water if it starts to dry out – it should be fairly sloppy. Serve with lots of fresh crispy salad and mashed potatoes (see page 187).

TIP To clean squid, pull the head away from the body – all the guts will slip out attached to the head. Cut between the eyes and tentacles. There is a crunchy bit between the tentacles, make sure this is removed. Keep the tentacles. Slice down the length of the body and remove any gooey bits and the quill, which is a transparent backbone. Remove the membrane from both sides of the body by scraping your knife over several times. Rinse well. Use only the tentacles and main body parts

CREOLE PRAWN AND CHICKEN GUMBO

Gumbo originates from Louisiana where the Mississippi river provides the wonderful fish and seafood associated with the state's cuisine. Its cultural diversity is reflected in the ingredients and cooking method of this dish.

TO SERVE FOUR TO SIX

4 tbsp corn oil
4 tbsp plain flour
2 whole chicken *cut into 8 pieces (about 1.5kg/3lb 5oz)*
3 tbsp dried thyme
400g/14oz black pudding *(or Portuguese or Spanish morcilla)*
2 onions *peeled and chopped*
1 red pepper *cored, de-seeded and chopped*
2 ribs of celery *cleaned, trimmed and chopped*
200g/7oz okra or ladies fingers *trimmed and chopped into 1cm/½in pieces*

3 tbsp dried oregano
3 tbsp dried oregano
1 red pepper *cored seeded and chopped*
4 cloves of garlic *peeled and chopped*
400g tin of chopped plum tomatoes
1 litre/1¾ pint prawn broth or fish stock
2 bay leaves
1 tbsp of Tabasco sauce
400g/14oz raw shelled prawns
1 large bunch fresh coriander *chopped*
salt and pepper

Preheat the oven to 150°C/300°F/gas mark 2. Heat 3 tablespoons of the oil in a very large pan on a medium heat and stir in 3 tablespoons of the flour. Leave to bubble without burning for 60 minutes, stirring frequently until the roux reaches a dark copper-colour, stirring frequently. Meanwhile, coat the chicken pieces in the rest of the flour and season with the thyme, salt and pepper. Heat the remaining oil in a very large frying pan and fry the chicken in batches until golden on both sides. Set aside.

Fry the black pudding in the same pan as the chicken and set aside until needed. Dump the onions and peppers in the pan and fry for about 10 minutes, or until beginning to soften. Stir in the other vegetables, the oregano and garlic, and continue frying for another 5 minutes. Transfer the vegetables into the roux and mix well. Continue cooking and stirring for 3 minutes, then add the tomatoes and stir until you have a thick sauce. Slowly stir in the stock, season with Tabasco, salt and pepper, and pop the chicken, prawns, black pudding and bay leaves into the pot. Stir through and place in the oven for 2 hours. Just before serving mix through the coriander. Serve with rice.

MOULES MARINIÈRES

Humans have been eating mussels for thousands of years and still continue to do so with slurps and glee – in Belgium and the Netherlands in particular, where they are likely to be served with chips and mayonnaise … perfection. This version is a really classic French dish, cooked in butter, wine, onions, parsley and cream. The delightful juices should be mopped up at the end of the meal with some crusty baguette. Extra bowls for shells and big napkins are always a good idea.

TO SERVE FOUR TO SIX

1kg/2¼lb mussels *scrubbed and beards removed*	175ml/6fl oz white wine
50g/2oz butter	200ml/7fl oz fish stock *(see page 185)*
4 shallots *peeled and finely chopped*	200ml/7fl oz double cream
1 pinch of saffron threads	1 bunch of fresh flat-leaf parsley *chopped*

Discard any mussels that don't close when tapped.

Melt the butter in a large pan with a lid and gently fry the shallots for 10 minutes, being careful not to brown them. Sprinkle in the saffron, splash in the wine and leave to simmer for another 10 minutes, or until all the wine has evaporated and the shallots are a wonderful golden brown colour.

Pour in the stock and bring to the boil, then dump in the mussels. Slam on the lid and give the pot a good shake. Simmer for 5 minutes, then take the mussels out of the pot, using tongs if you have them, and pop into a bowl. Bin any that have not opened fully.

Glug the cream into the soup and scatter in the parsley, then heat through and gently simmer for 5 minutes. Put the mussels back in the pan, shake once more with the lid on, heat for a couple of minutes, then ladle into bowls, dividing the soup evenly between them. Serve with crusty bread.

VEGETABLE SOUPS

LEEK AND POTATO SOUP

SEEDED ROLLS

Antony Worrall Thompson's
WHITE BEAN AND BUTTERNUT SQUASH SOUP

WATERCRESS SOUP

SOUPE AU PISTOU

ROOT SOUP

BORSCHT

ONION SOUP

CREAM OF TOMATO SOUP

GAZPACHO

Mark Broadbent's
NETTLE SOUP

VEGETABLE STEWS

AUBERGINE STEW WITH FRIED HALLOUMI AND WALNUTS

BUTTERNUT SQUASH AND GOAT'S CHEESE STEW

BLACK BEAN AND RED PEPPER STEW

CHORIZO AND BUTTER BEAN STEW

CAPONATA

MELANZANE ALLA PARMIGIANA

RATATOUILLE

IMAM BAYALDI WITH DILL RICE

Vegetables

LEEK AND POTATO SOUP

As an ode to the humble potato, I have made a delicious leek and potato soup: it is filling, inexpensive and simple. As it comprises mainly just veg – leeks and potatoes – you should buy the best-quality veg you can find. Home grown is always best. For a vegetarian option, leave out the bacon.

TO SERVE FOUR

a drizzle of olive oil
150g/5oz bacon lardons (optional)
500g/1lb 2oz leeks *(about 5 medium leeks) cleaned, trimmed and chopped*
500g/1lb 2oz potatoes *(about 6 medium potatoes) peeled and cut into small cubes*

150ml/5fl oz double cream *(Jersey would be best)*
½ tsp freshly grated nutmeg
1 handful of chopped fresh flat-leaf parsley
sea salt and freshly ground black pepper
seeded rolls *(see over) to serve*

Heat the oil in a large pan over a medium heat and fry the lardons, if using, until beginning to brown. Dump in the vegetables and season with a little salt and pepper. Cover with water, turn up the heat a little and leave to boil for 15 minutes, or until the potatoes are starting to fall apart.

Stir in the cream, nutmeg and parsley, and season with plenty of salt and pepper. Heat through and serve with warm seeded rolls.

TIP The best potatoes to use are the floury varieties such as Maris Piper or King Edward as they will become soften and thicken the soup. Waxy potatoes hold their shape and are too firm for the job.

SEEDED ROLLS — MAKES TWELVE SMALL ROLLS

500g/1lb 2oz plain white flour *plus extra to dust*
2 tsp caster sugar
2 tsp salt
50g/2oz butter *plus extra to grease*

1 handful each sesame seeds, linseeds
and sunflower seeds
2 tsp dried yeast
300ml/10fl oz warm water

Mix the flour, sugar and salt together, then rub in the butter. Stir in the seeds and dried yeast and gradually mix in the warm water until you have a soft dough.

Turn out onto a floured surface and knead for 10 minutes.

Grease a baking tray. Divide the dough into 12 balls and pop onto the baking tray. Don't crowd them too much as the little darlings will grow. Cover with a clean tea towel and leave in a warm place for 1½ hours or until doubled in size.

Preheat the oven to 200°C/400°F/gas mark 6.

Slide the tray into the oven on the middle runner and cook for 20 minutes or until the rolls sound hollow when tapped on the bottom. Cool on a wire rack.

Antony Worrall Thompson's
WHITE BEAN AND BUTTERNUT SQUASH SOUP

A lovely winter warmer. Squash and beans make a surprisingly delicious partnership.

TO SERVE FOUR TO SIX

For the soup
1kg/2¼lb butternut squash *seeded and each half cut into wedges*
4 tbsp good olive oil
2 onions *peeled and finely diced*
2 carrots *peeled and cut into 1cm/½ inch dice*
2 ribs of celery *cleaned, trimmed and cut into 1cm/½ inch dice*
6 cloves of garlic *peeled*
1 tbsp finely chopped fresh sage
1.5 litres/2½ pints vegetable stock

2 x 400g tins of white beans *rinsed and drained*
sea salt and freshly ground black pepper

For the parsley purée
2 cloves of garlic *peeled*
1 tsp sea salt
1 bunch of fresh flat-leaf parsley *finely chopped*
4 tbsp freshly grated Parmesan
4 tbsp good olive oil
lemon juice to taste

Preheat the oven to 180°C/350°F/gas mark 4. Place the squash in a roasting tray with 1 tablespoon of the oil and roast for about 45 minutes or until the squash has softened and caramelised. Leave to cool a little, then remove the flesh from the skin.

While the squash is cooking, heat the remaining oil in a large pan and cook the onions, carrots, celery, garlic and sage over a medium heat until the onions are soft but not brown. Add the stock and bring to the boil, then simmer for 20 minutes. Add the roasted squash and half the beans and cook for a further 10 minutes. Place the soup and beans in a liquidiser and blend until smooth. Return to the pan, add the remaining beans, carefully stir to combine, and season to taste.

To make the parsley purée, blend the garlic, salt, parsley and Parmesan in a liquidiser then drizzle in the olive oil. Add lemon juice to taste. Serve a teaspoonful of parsley purée in each bowl of the hot soup.

WATERCRESS SOUP

The colour of this luscious soup always thrills me – it is an unbelievably vivid green. It is also extremely delicious made with spinach.

TO SERVE EIGHT

400g/14oz fresh watercress *cleaned*
50g/2oz butter
1 onion *peeled and chopped*
3 leeks *cleaned, trimmed and chopped*
2 ribs of celery *cleaned and chopped*

1 tbsp plain flour
600ml/1 pint good chicken stock *(see page 185)*
300ml/10fl oz double cream
a grating of nutmeg
sea salt

Pour 500ml/18fl oz of salted water into a pan and bring to the boil. Dump in the watercress and move it about with a spoon until it is all submerged in the water. Leave to boil for 10 minutes. Remove from the heat to cool.

Meanwhile, heat another large pot on a low to medium heat, add the butter, onion, leeks and celery and gently stew for 10 minutes.

Sprinkle the flour into the onion pot and stir for a couple of minutes, then slowly add the stock, a ladleful at a time, stirring as the sauce thickens. Once all the stock has been incorporated, leave to bubble for 5 minutes.

Return to the watercress, which should be cool, and pour it, water and all, into a blender. Whiz until smooth. Next, pour the onion mixture and the cream into the blender with the watercress and whiz again until velvety.

Return the soup to the pot, season with salt and nutmeg, heat through and serve.

SOUPE AU PISTOU

My parents bought a stunning farm deep in the countryside of Provence when I was a teenager. With only snakes, lizards and frogs as neighbours, it was a rural paradise. The local butcher was exceptional and the markets were cornucopias of deliciousness. I first tasted this exquisite soup at the local bistro, now rather famous for its outstanding food. I wrestled the recipe from the maître d', who scribbled the ingredients and an incoherent method on a piece of paper. Simple, fresh and totally wonderful, it can be made with other beans, vegetables and a variety of pastas. My kids' favourite is with alphabetti spaghetti.

TO SERVE EIGHT

200g/7oz dried borlotti or haricot beans *soaked overnight* or 1½ tins of borlotti or haricot beans *drained*
1 rib of celery *cleaned and trimmed*
4 ripe tomatoes *peeled, seeded and cut into quarters (see page 121)*
1 bunch of fresh flat-leaf parsley
1 large carrot *peeled*
1 head of garlic *cut in half*
2 tbsp olive oil *plus extra to serve*
150g/5oz French beans *cut into 2cm/¾ inch pieces*

3 carrots *peeled and cut into 1cm/½ inch cubes*
2 courgettes *cleaned, trimmed and cut into 1cm/½ inch cubes*
2 handfuls of elbow macaroni
sea salt and freshly ground black pepper

For the pistou
75g/3oz freshly grated Parmesan
4 fat cloves of garlic *peeled*
1 large bunch of fresh basil *stalks and all*
2 tbsp olive oil

Drain and rinse the soaked beans. Boil the beans rapidly for 10 minutes in plenty of water, then drain. Return them to the pot with water to come about 10cm/4 inches above the beans. Add the celery, 1 tomato, the parsley, carrot, garlic and a little salt and boil for 1¼ hours. Remove the boiled herbs, veg and garlic and discard. If using tinned beans, dollop them into a large pot and cover with 750ml/1¾ pints of water and bring to the boil. Stir in the oil, the chopped vegetables and seasoning. Top up with more water if it looks a bit dry. Bring to the boil and simmer for a further 20 minutes. Add the pasta and cook until tender.

Meanwhile, make the pistou. Put the Parmesan in a blender, add the garlic and basil and whiz to combine, then drizzle in the oil and whiz to a chunky sauce. Serve the soup with a dollop of the pistou on top and a little more olive oil.

ROOT SOUP

This is easy to throw together, and is usually made from whatever I find in the vegetable drawer at the bottom of the fridge, plus any spices I am in the mood for. This soup is a great way to get a big dose of vegetables: it is soothing, satisfying and worthy of poetry.

TO SERVE FOUR

250g/9oz carrots *peeled and chopped*
250g/9oz sweet potatoes *peeled and chopped*
250g/9oz parsnips *peeled and chopped*
1½ tsp cumin seeds
1½ tsp crushed dried chilli
3 tbsp olive oil

25g/1oz butter
150g/5oz red onions *peeled and chopped*
150g/5oz celery *cleaned, trimmed and chopped*
1 large leek *cleaned, trimmed and chopped*
sea salt and freshly ground black pepper

Preheat the oven to 190°C/370°F/gas mark 5. Put half the carrots aside and put the rest of the carrots, the sweet potatoes and parsnips in a baking tray. Add the spices, salt and pepper and 2 tablespoons of the oil and shake the tray until all the vegetables are coated with oil. Place in the middle of the oven for up to 45 minutes, checking and turning from time to time until they are soft and browned.

Meanwhile, heat the remaining oil and the butter in a large pan with a lid. Add the onions and cook on a gentle heat until translucent – about 5 minutes.

Add the remaining carrots, the celery and leek to the onions and grind over some pepper. Cover the pan and cook for 20 minutes, stirring occasionally to make sure the vegetables do not burn or stick to the pan. If the mixture becomes watery, uncover the pan until all the liquid has evaporated.

Add 1.5 litres/2½ pints water, the roast vegetables and plenty of salt and simmer for a further 10 minutes. Remove from the heat and leave to cool a little, then whiz in a blender until smooth. Try serving with warm, buttered cheese scones.

BORSCHT

Borscht is an Eastern European vegetable soup where beetroot is the main ingredient and it is, therefore, a fabulous red colour. Each Eastern European country seems to have a slight variation on the recipe; the Ukraine and Belarus, for example, always use tomatoes, and in Russia, meat is often added. It does not even always have beetroot, but seems in some countries to mean just soup. Rudolf Nureyev, Russia's most famous ballet dancer, had his own Borscht recipe – his version involved meat, tomatoes, lemon and sugar and no beetroot.

TO SERVE FOUR TO SIX

1 red onion *peeled*
2 carrots *peeled*
3 beetroot *peeled*
2 ribs of celery *cleaned, trimmed and finely chopped*
1 leek *cleaned, trimmed and finely chopped*
150g/5oz butter
3 cloves of garlic *peeled and finely chopped*

1 tsp caraway seeds
1 tbsp tomato purée
1 litre/1¾ pints vegetable stock
1 bay leaf
150ml/5fl oz soured cream, to serve
sea salt and freshly ground black pepper

Either finely chop the onion, carrots and beetroot, or grate them in a food processor. Put all the vegetables in a large pan with the butter, garlic, caraway seeds and a grind of black pepper.

Fry gently for 15 minutes until soft, stirring often and reducing the heat if it looks like it might burn.

Stir in the tomato purée, stock and bay leaf, season with salt and bring to a gentle boil, then simmer for 1 hour.

Cool the soup a little, then whiz in a blender until smooth. Pour back into the pan and heat through, and serve with a dollop of soured cream on top.

ONION SOUP

Onion soups have been popular since Roman times at least. As recipe-creation legends go, this one is highly improbable: the soup was created by King Louis XV of France. One night he arrived at his hunting lodge to discover he had only onions, butter and champagne and, voilà, the first onion soup was created. (Considering that, at the French court at Versailles, the king's dining table was over a trapdoor so that food would mysteriously appear and disappear in front of the spoilt king, it is unlikely that he had ever entered a kitchen, let alone invented recipes.)

TO SERVE FOUR TO SIX

100g/3½oz butter
4 onions *peeled and sliced*
3 cloves of garlic *peeled and chopped*
1 tbsp raw cane sugar
1 tsp each finely chopped fresh rosemary
and thyme
175ml/6fl oz wine *white, red or* champagne
1.5 litres/2½ pints good beef stock *(see page 184)*

150g/5oz Gruyère cheese
sea salt and freshly ground black pepper

For the croutons
½ baguette *cut into 2cm/¾ inch slices*
2 cloves of garlic *peeled*

Melt the butter in a large pan, add the onions and stew for 20 minutes until soft, stirring every now and then. Turn up the heat and throw in the garlic, stirring for 2 minutes, then stir in the sugar, herbs and wine. Reduce the heat and simmer for another 30 minutes, stirring every now and then until the onions are nice and caramelised. Preheat the oven to 150°C/300°F/gas mark 2. Add the stock to the pan and pop into the oven for 3 hours. About 20 minutes before the end of the cooking time, arrange the slices of bread on a baking tray and put into the oven to bake. Take the bread and soup out of the oven together and season the soup to taste. Turn on the grill. Ladle the soup into ovenproof bowls. Make sure not to over-fill the bowls, as removing them from the grill could be difficult without suffering scalds. Rub the slices of bread with garlic and pop on top of the soup. Grate over a good covering of cheese and place the bowls on a baking tray. Grill until the cheese is bubbling and browned. Serve hot.

CREAM OF TOMATO SOUP

In our house when we were growing up, if we were ill in bed we would always have a tray brought up with Heinz tomato soup and toast. I still love a bowl of Heinz when I am feeling under the weather. However, this gorgeous orange soup is even better. It's fresh and creamy and just hits the yum spot. Try it with a little basil, dill, mint or tarragon stirred in at the end, or just with a beautiful swirl of extra cream.

TO SERVE SIX

20 ripe tomatoes
125g/4oz butter
2 large onions *peeled and chopped*

200ml/7fl oz double cream
sea salt and freshly ground black pepper

Bring a large pan of water to the boil, then remove from the heat. Drop the tomatoes in and leave to stand for 2–3 minutes or until the skins split when poked with a sharp knife. Strain and remove to a large bowl to cool.

Clean the pan quickly and drop in the butter and onions in a pan for 10 minutes. Sauté gently for 10 minutes. Meanwhile, using 2 bowls – one for the tomatoes and one for reserving all the pips and skins, peel the tomatoes, squeeze out the pips and cut off the tough green bit where the stalk was attached. Put the tomato quarters into the pan with the onions and season with pepper. Simmer for 5 minutes.

Squeeze the tomato pips and skins to release the juices, then strain into the pan using a fine-meshed sieve. Use the back of your spoon to squeeze the juice out of the pips, by pressing against the side of the sieve and stirring. Simmer for a further 15 minutes.

Blend in the cream and a little water if needed and adjust the seasoning to taste. Serve with crusty bread.

GAZPACHO

Gazpacho is a Spanish, chilled summer soup for hot days and is one of my favourite soups. It can be made very complicated, but I like this simple vegetable smoothie-style recipe, which takes just 15 minutes to throw together. Really big tasty tomatoes from a farmers' market in August would be my ultimate choice.

TO SERVE TWO TO FOUR

1 piece of stale ciabatta the size of your fist
2 tbsp red wine vinegar
½ cucumber *peeled and chopped*
1 small red pepper *cored, seeded and chopped*
1 mild red chilli *cut in half lengthways, seeded and roughly chopped and cubed (optional)*

3 big, ripe tomatoes *peeled and seeded (see page 121)*
3 spring onions *trimmed and roughly chopped*
2 cloves of garlic *peeled and roughly chopped*
1 handful of crushed ice
2 tbsp olive oil
sea salt and freshly ground black pepper

Crumble the bread into a bowl. Pour the vinegar over it and work the bread in with your fingers. Chop some of cucumber, red pepper and tomatoes into little cubes if you want to add them into each bowl at the end for a little texture. Put all the ingredients except the oil into a blender and pulse until smooth. Season to taste.

Serve with a few cubed vegetables on top if you are using them, and a drizzle of oil.

Mark Broadbent's
NETTLE SOUP

Mark is the sensational chef who oversees the team at the Bluebird. He has helped bring English cuisine's reputation back from the doldrums. This soup was traditionally served as a spring tonic using early-season, tender young nettles which are full of vitamins and minerals.

TO SERVE FOUR

600g/1lb 5oz stinging nettle leaves
50g/2oz unsalted butter
400g/14oz leeks *cleaned, trimmed and finely sliced*
175g/6oz onions *peeled and finely sliced*

175g/6oz potatoes *peeled and finely diced*
500ml/18fl oz water
500ml/18fl oz milk
crème fraîche *to serve*

Blanch the stinging nettles (being very careful not to sting yourself – a good, clean pair of rubber or gardening gloves will come in very handy) in boiling water for 2–3 minutes. Drain and refresh in iced water. Drain again and set aside.

Melt the butter in a large pan, and sweat the leeks and onions without colouring them for about 10 minutes. Add the potatoes and cook for a further few minutes.

In another pan, bring the milk and water up to the boil, then pour over the vegetables and simmer rapidly for 8 minutes.

Whiz the mixture in a food processor, or use a hand blender, add the blanched nettles and blend again. Pass through a fine sieve and reheat gently. To serve, pour the soup into 4 bowls and add a spoonful of crème fraîche to the centre of each one.

AUBERGINE STEW WITH FRIED HALLOUMI AND WALNUTS

This delicious recipe makes a fabulous vegetarian dish or part of a big lunch party, preferably in a Mediterranean garden with butterflies, grilled lamb, couscous and friends.

TO SERVE FOUR TO SIX

4 tbsp olive oil
50g/2oz butter
300g/11oz red onions *peeled and chopped*
3 cloves of garlic *peeled and finely chopped*
400g tin of chopped tomatoes
1 tsp ground cumin
2 tsp golden caster sugar

300g/11oz aubergines *trimmed and cut into bite-sized pieces*
1 good handful of pine nuts or walnuts
175g/6oz good-quality halloumi cheese
1 handful of chopped fresh mint
sea salt and freshly ground black pepper
1 handful of chopped fresh coriander, *to garnish*

Heat 2 teaspoons of the oil and the butter in a large frying pan. Add the onions and cook over a gentle heat for 15 minutes. Stir in the garlic and cook for 2 minutes, then stir in the tomatoes, cumin and sugar and take off the heat.

Heat all but ½ tablespoon of the remaining oil in a clean pan, add the aubergines and fry until golden and thoroughly cooked. Stir in the tomato mixture and the nuts and heat through, then season to taste.

Slice the halloumi into 5mm/¼ inch slices and fry in the remaining oil until golden on both sides. Stir the mint into the aubergines, pour into a serving dish and pop the warm halloumi on top.

Sprinkle over the coriander and serve with a big herby green salad, and sourdough toast or toasted wholemeal pitta.

BUTTERNUT SQUASH AND GOAT'S CHEESE STEW

This simple dish gets the thumbs up from all who have tried it for its sheer yumminess. Try topped with other cheeses too – Roquefort or mozzarella work superbly.

TO SERVE SIX

3 tbsp olive oil
50g/2oz butter
2 onions *peeled and sliced*
2 fat cloves of garlic *peeled and chopped*
2 tsp each finely chopped fresh thyme
and rosemary
1 butternut squash *peeled, seeded and cubed*
1 small sweet potato *peeled and cubed*

150ml/5fl oz white wine
4 tomatoes *peeled, seeded and cut in half (see page 121)*
150ml/5fl oz vegetable stock
100ml/3½fl oz double cream
200g/7oz goat's cheese *preferably a nice, firm goat's cheese log with rind, sliced*
sea salt and freshly ground black pepper

Heat the oil and butter in a large pan on a medium heat. Bung in the onions and gently fry for about 10 minutes or until soft.

Stir in the garlic, thyme and rosemary, followed by the squash and sweet potato. Season with salt and plenty of pepper and continue cooking for 15 minutes, stirring often.

Stir in the wine and turn up the heat for a couple of minutes, so the wine reduces by half. Reduce the heat, plop in the tomatoes, then glug in the stock. Stir and boil gently for a further 10 minutes, or until all the veg are lovely and soft and cooked to taste. Season with salt and pepper. Preheat the grill.

Stir through the cream and place the cheese on top of the stew. Pop under the grill until all the cheese has melted and started to brown. Serve with couscous and a crunchy green salad.

BLACK BEAN AND RED PEPPER STEW

A scrumptious vegetarian bean dish with heaps of flavour. Fab as a main course, or as part of a picnic.

TO SERVE FOUR AS A MAIN — EIGHT AS A SIDE

300g/11oz dried black beans *soaked overnight*
1 rib of celery *cleaned and trimmed*
1 leek *cleaned and trimmed*
1 carrot *peeled*
1 tomato
1 head of garlic, *cut in half horizontally*
1 bunch of fresh flat-leaf parsley
1 red pepper
340g tin of sweetcorn kernels

1 tsp dried cumin
1 large mild chilli *cut in half lengthways, seeded and chopped*
2 cloves of garlic *peeled and finely chopped*
grated zest and juice of 1 lemon
2 tbsp olive oil
1 large bunch of fresh mint *chopped*
sea salt and freshly ground black pepper

Drain and rinse the beans and pour into a large pan. Cover with water, bring to the boil and boil vigorously for 10 minutes. Drain, rinse and return to the pan with the celery, leek, carrot, tomato, garlic, parsley and salt to taste. Return to the heat and gently boil for 1 hour or until tender.

Meanwhile, using tongs, put the red pepper over a gas flame and turn it until charred and blackened all over. Pop into a bowl until it is cool enough to handle, then peel off the skin, discard the seeds, stalk and skin and slice into strips.

Drain the beans and discard the bits and bobs they have been boiling with. Put the beans back into the pan. Take out 2 tablespoons of the beans and purée them, then stir back into the pan along with the corn, cumin, chilli, garlic, lemon zest and juice, the oil, three-quarters of the pepper slices and three-quarters of the mint. Season to taste. Lay the remaining strips of red pepper on top, sprinkle with the remaining mint and serve hot or cold.

Great with rice or couscous and buttered French beans.

CHORIZO AND BUTTER BEAN STEW

There are few things more wholesome and nourishing than a big bowl of this stew. It is perfect for a cold winter evening.

TO SERVE SIX

400g/14oz Spanish chorizo *skinned and sliced*
2 tbsp oil
1 onion *peeled and chopped*
3 cloves of garlic *peeled, halved and crushed with the side of a knife*
1 dried chilli *crushed*

1 handful of chopped fresh sage leaves
2 x 400g tins of butter beans *drained (reserve the liquid from one tin)*
100ml/3½fl oz good beef or chicken stock *(see pages 184 and 185)*
sea salt and freshly ground black pepper

Fry the chorizo in the oil in a large pan until beginning to crisp. Dump in the onion and stew for 5 minutes, then stir in the garlic, chilli and sage and continue cooking slowly for 20 minutes or until the onion is soft.

Mash half a tin of beans with a little of its liquid or water in a pestle and mortar. Add the mashed beans, the remaining beans and the stock to the pan, stir through and season with salt and pepper.

Simmer for 10 minutes, stirring often, and serve with fried potatoes and salad.

CAPONATA

Caponata is a classic Sicilian stew dating back to Roman times. As with all ancient dishes, the ingredients vary from one recipe to another – it is said that there are more than thirty-seven different recipes to be found on Sicily alone. It is mostly served as a side dish, dip, or appetiser these days, but when it appeared in records, from the 1700s, it was eaten as a main course. It is delicious served with grilled polenta.

TO SERVE TWO AS A MAIN – FOUR AS A STARTER/SIDE

olive oil
2 aubergines *trimmed and diced*
1 onion *peeled and chopped*
2 ribs of celery *cleaned, trimmed and chopped*
1 tsp ground cinnamon
50ml/2fl oz sherry vinegar
½ tbsp raw cane sugar

1 tbsp pine nuts
1 tbsp black olives *stoned and chopped*
1 tbsp capers
200g/7oz tomatoes *peeled, seeded and chopped* (*see page 121*)
25g/1oz fresh basil *plus a few leaves for the top*
sea salt and freshly ground black pepper

Heat a good glug of oil – about 4 tablespoons – in a large pan on a medium to high heat.

Dump in the aubergines and fry, stirring all the time, until soft and browned – about 10 minutes. Reduce the heat slightly, then throw in the onion and celery and stir through. Add a little more oil if needed, grind in some black pepper and sprinkle over the cinnamon. Fry for a further 10 minutes, stirring often.

Pour in the vinegar, sprinkle in the sugar, pop in the pine nuts, olives and capers and fry for a further 5 minutes, stirring continuously.

Add the tomatoes and basil, stir and simmer for the last 10 minutes. Season to taste and serve with rice or couscous for a main dish, or grilled polenta squares as a starter.

MELANZANE ALLA PARMIGIANA

Melanzane alla Parmigiana is one of the most famous dishes from Naples. It is made with aubergines, tomato sauce, mozzarella and Parmesan in layers and then baked. The simple tomato sauce is simmered for quite a long time, making it rich and delicious. The type of aubergines available today do not need salting to remove the bitterness since they are hybrids and the bitterness has been bred out of them by clever horticulturalists.

TO SERVE FOUR AS A MAIN — SIX AS A STARTER/SIDE

2 aubergines *trimmed and sliced into discs as thick as your thumb*
1 tbsp plain flour
4 tbsp olive oil
1 bunch of fresh basil *chopped*
400g/14oz mozzarella
125g/4oz freshly grated Parmesan

For the tomato sauce
2 tbsp olive oil
50g/2oz butter
1 onion *peeled and chopped*
8 ripe tomatoes *peeled, seeded and cut into quarters (see page 121)*
sea salt and freshly ground black pepper

First make the tomato sauce. Heat the oil and butter in a pan and fry the onion on a lowish heat for about 10 minutes until softened, stirring every now and then. Plop in all the tomatoes and continue cooking for 30 minutes, stirring and mashing up the tomatoes with your spoon occasionally. Season to taste.

Preheat the oven to 180°C/350°F/gas mark 4. Dust the aubergines with flour. Heat half the oil in a large pan until smoking. Place a few of the aubergines in to cover the base of the pan in one layer and fry until deep golden on both sides. The aubergines are a little bit like sponges and will soak up all the oil quickly so you may need to squeeze them with your spoon or tongs a bit to release some of the oil back into the pan. Fry the remaining aubergines in the rest of the oil and transfer to a plate lined with absorbent kitchen paper. Season them with a little salt and pepper. Layer the components into an ovenproof dish, starting with some of the aubergines, then a layer of tomato sauce and a sprinkling of basil, followed by mozzarella. Scatter over some Parmesan and continue to layer, finishing with Parmesan as the final layer, for a lovely, crisp, golden top. Slide into the oven and bake for 30 minutes.

RATATOUILLE

I love this version of ratatouille, as all the veg are cooked separately and quickly so that the flavours of each are fresh and defined. The name comes from the French verb 'touiller', which means 'to toss'. Originally the vegetables tossed together were tomatoes, courgettes, peppers, onions and garlic, without aubergine, which was not available at the same time of year as the other veg.

TO SERVE FOUR AS A MAIN — SIX AS A SIDE

3 peppers *1 red, 1 yellow and 1 orange*
4 tbsp olive oil
2 aubergines *trimmed and sliced in discs as thick as your thumb, ends discarded*
1 tbsp plain flour
3 courgettes *trimmed and cut into sticks*
1 large onion *peeled and chopped*

4 cloves of garlic *peeled and chopped*
1 tsp finely chopped fresh thyme leaves
8 ripe tomatoes *peeled, seeded and cut into quarters* (*see page 121*)
1 handful of basil basil
sea salt and freshly ground black pepper

Preheat the oven to 220°C/425°F/gas mark 7. Put the whole peppers on an ovenproof tray and pop in the oven for 30 minutes until they are soft and blackened. Remove to a plate and leave to cool. Meanwhile, heat about 3 tablespoons of the oil in a large pan until smoking. Dust the aubergines in the flour, place them in the pan in one layer and fry until golden on both sides. Remove and drain on some absorbent kitchen paper.

Heat another glug of oil until simmering. Fry the courgette pieces until golden on all sides. Remove from the pan and set aside with the aubergines. Reduce the heat, toss in the onion and gently fry for 10 minutes, stirring frequently. Stir in the garlic, thyme and plenty of pepper then cook gently for 5 minutes, then add the tomatoes. Mash the tomatoes with your wooden spoon until they collapse into a pulp, then add salt to taste and simmer for 15 minutes.

While the tomatoes are simmering, slip the skins off the peppers, discard the seeds and core and tear the flesh into strips. Toss all the vegetables and basil into the tomatoes. Season to taste. Serve hot or cold.

IMAM BAYALDI WITH DILL RICE

Imam Bayaldi quite literally means 'the cleric fainted' – presumably from the sheer exquisite deliciousness of the dish.

TO SERVE FOUR

2 large aubergines *trimmed and pricked*
4 tbsp olive oil
2 red onions *peeled and chopped*
4 cloves of garlic *peeled and sliced*
3 tsp ground cumin
1 heaped tsp cinnamon
1½ tsp brown sugar
1 handful of almonds
1 handful of raisins
4 ripe tomatoes *peeled and chopped (see page 121)*
1 handful of chopped fresh mint leaves *chopped*

1 handful of chopped fresh coriander leaves *chopped*
sea salt and freshly ground black pepper
plain yoghurt, *to serve*

For the Dill Rice
1 handful of basmati rice per person *plus 1 for the pot*
¾ chicken stock cube
50g/2oz butter
1 large handful of chopped fresh dill
sea salt and freshly ground black pepper

Preheat the oven to 220°C/425°F/gas mark 7. Put the aubergines on an ovenproof tray and bake them in the oven for 25 minutes. Meanwhile, heat half the oil in an ovenproof pan and gently fry the onions until soft. Sprinkle in the garlic, spices, sugar, nuts and raisins. Give it a good stir and cook for a further 10 minutes, stirring often.

Once it is baked, scoop out the aubergine flesh, chop, and add to the pan with the rest of the oil and the tomatoes. Continue cooking and stirring until the stew thickens slightly. Season to taste. Turn down the oven to 150°C/300°F/gas mark 2 and pop the pan in for 30 minutes. Meanwhile, prepare the dill rice by placing the rice in a sieve and rinse with water. Bring the kettle to the boil and dissolve the chicken stock cube in boiling water in a mug. Put the rice in a pan with a lid, along with the chicken stock and a pinch of salt and add more cold water. Pop the pan on a medium heat with the lid on until all the liquid has been absorbed, about 20 minutes, but check it has not boiled dry and add a little more water if needed. Don't stir it until it is cooked. Fork through the butter and dill and season to taste. Remove the stew from the oven and stir through the chopped herbs. Serve with the rice and a dollop of yoghurt.

MAKING STOCK

BEEF STOCK

LAMB STOCK

CHICKEN STOCK

FISH STOCK

COOKING
BEANS AND PULSES

MANY WAYS
WITH POTATOES

MASHED POTATOES

RÖSTI

POMMES DAUPHINOISES

ROSEMARY ROAST NEW POTATOES

Useful Extras

MAKING STOCK

I am afraid to say that I am one of those sad people who makes their own stock. I watched my mother do it and it has always seemed quite natural to use up the leftover roast to make something tasty, versatile and useful. I do get teased though. I freeze my stock in different sized tubs, the little ones for gravy and the larger ones for soups, stews, risottos, and so on. I have learned a thing or two about stock-making and the gist is this:

1 It never tastes the same twice.

2 Leaving it on the stove while you go out with friends is a catastrophically bad idea since, when the liquid evaporates, the bones begin to burn and after a few hours the smell seeps into every nook and cranny of the house and stays there for days. It is without a doubt one of the worst smells you will ever encounter. So, unless you are particularly peeved with your housemates, always keep a tiny corner of your eye on the pot.

3 Lemons, garlic, rosemary and thyme do not improve the stock. I usually stuff my roast chicken with a selection of the above and have found removing them before placing the carcass in the stockpot gives a smoother, less bitter or woody taste.

4 Leftover roast vegetables do improve the flavour, especially the sweet ones like parsnips, carrots, sweet potatoes and squash.

5 Do add raw parsley, tarragon, onion, celery or celeriac, leek and carrots to the pot; the better cleaned and trimmed, the better the stock.

6 Leftover gravy finds a new lease of life in stock (but it will make it cloudy).

7 The more meat on the carcass, the better.

8 Over-boiled stock tastes rough.

DOS AND DON'TS

• Do add wine, red or white. Port and sherry are fab too. Alcohol should probably not constitute more than a fifth of the liquid, the rest being water.

• Don't use oily fish for your fish stock, although a little salmon is okay.

• Do simmer the stock gently, so it just quivers. Do not simmer meat with small bones and veg stocks for more than 2 hours, as the flavour has come out of the meat and bones by then and you will get a musty bone flavour. Yuck. Fish stock takes only 45 minutes. The larger the bones, the longer the cooking.

• Do taste your stock using a spoon, and sprinkle with a tiny amount of salt. It should be a delicious broth and heaven on its own.

• Do remove the bits, bones and bobs from the stock asap. Do not leave them in your precious juice too long after it has come off the stove, as it will spoil it well and proper.

• Once the stock is done, it may still be a little insipid in flavour. So, after removing the bones, herbs and veg, return the stock to the heat to reduce. This can be done at a rolling boil.

• Do show your friends' children what you are cooking – they will think you are a witch and will behave in your house.

• Do freeze your stock in ice cube containers. It is great to pop the frozen chunks into gravy, soup, and so on. Watch them melt as you stir.

• Don't listen to me – have a go yourself. Anything with bones and meat make good stock.

NOTE In some of the kitchens of yesteryear, legend has it that they would have a huge stockpot into which any leftover gubbins would be dropped: it was constantly topped up with wine dregs, veg peelings and water and never turned off or replaced. Yikes, I think today's health and safety inspector would have passed out.

BEEF STOCK — MAKES ABOUT 2 LITRES/3.5 PINTS

1 calf knuckle
600g/1lb 5oz beef shin *bone in*
2 carrots *peeled*
1 leek *cleaned and trimmed*

½ large onion *peeled*
1 rib of celery *cleaned and trimmed*
1 sprig of fresh flat-leaf parsley
100ml/3½fl oz sherry or white wine

Put all the ingredients in a large pot, cover with water and simmer very gently for 4 hours, scooping off and discarding any scum that rises to the surface.

Strain the precious liquid and bin all the gubbins. Cool and then refrigerate for up to 5 days, until needed. Skim off any fat and use the stock for a billion tasty dishes. Can be frozen for up to 3 months.

LAMB STOCK — MAKES ABOUT 2 LITRES/3.5 PINTS

500g/1lb 2oz lamb breast *bones in*
2 carrots *peeled*
1 leek *cleaned, trimmed and cut in half*
1 onion *peeled and stuck with 2 cloves*

1 bunch of fresh flat-leaf parsley
2 mushrooms *trimmed*
150ml/5fl oz white wine

Put all the ingredients in a large pot, cover with water and very gently simmer for 3 hours, scooping off and discarding any scum that rises to the surface.

Strain the stock, chuck out all the veg and gubbins (the meat is quite tasty if you feel like eating it, otherwise give it to a hungry dog). Bring the liquid to the boil and reduce by half. Cool and then refrigerate for up to 5 days, until needed. Skim off any fat before using. Can be frozen for up to 3 months.

CHICKEN STOCK — MAKES ABOUT 2 LITRES/3.5 PINTS

1 whole chicken, cut into four pieces, a leftover chicken carcass from a roast, or 6 chicken thighs
2 carrots *peeled*
1 small onion *peeled and cut in half*

1 leek *cleaned, trimmed and cut in half*
2 ribs of celery *cleaned, trimmed and cut in half*
1 small bunch of fresh flat-leaf parsley

Put all the ingredients into a large pan with a lid and cover with water. Cover the pan and set on a low heat to very gently simmer for 1 hour, or until the chicken is cooked through, or up to 2 hours if you are using a chicken carcass. Scoop off and discard any scum that rises to the surface. Remove the chicken pieces and set aside on a plate.

Discard the vegetables, parsley and chicken carcass, if using. Keep the chicken meat for soup, sandwiches, salads or chicken pie. Strain the stock into a bowl to cool, then refrigerate for up to five days, until needed. Skim off any fat before using. Can be frozen for up to three months.

FISH STOCK — MAKES ABOUT 2 LITRES/3.5 PINTS

500g/1lb 2oz fish bones and skin *(ask your fishmonger for the trimmings)*
1 onion *peeled and cut in half*
1 carrot *peeled*
1 rib of celery *cleaned and trimmed*

1 bunch of fresh dill
fennel trimmings
2 litres/3½ pints water
150ml/5fl oz white wine or Pernod

Put everything in a large pan and simmer on a low heat for 45 minutes, without allowing it to boil. Scoop off and discard any scum that rises to the surface.

Remove the bones, skin and vegetables, then strain the stock. Cool and then refrigerate for up to 5 days, until needed. Can be frozen for up to 3 months.

COOKING
BEANS AND PULSES

Beans and pulses are inexpensive, very healthy and convenient, not much harder to cook than making a cup of tea. This is my rough guide to cooking dried beans once they have been soaked overnight, such as borlotti, kidney, black beans, pinto beans, butter beans, chickpeas and black-eyed peas. Lentils and split peas don't need soaking.

To cook the beans, place them in a pan and generously cover with water. Bring to a rapid boil for 10 minutes, then drain and rinse.

Pop them back in the pan with a 2cm x 10cm/ ¾ inch x 4 inch piece of bacon rind (optional), half a head of garlic cut horizontally (skin on), 2 small carrots, peeled, 1 leek, cleaned and trimmed, a little bunch of fresh parsley and a whole tomato.

Cover with plenty of water (about 5cm/2 inches above the beans) and bring to a gentle boil for 1½ hours. They can now be used in soups, stews, salads or any other dish you can dream up.

MANY WAYS WITH POTATOES

Potatoes are the ideal accompaniment to stews; here are some classic potato recipes.

MASHED POTATOES — TO SERVE FOUR TO SIX

6 medium-sized Maris Piper potatoes *peeled and cubed*
75ml/3fl oz milk

50g/2oz butter
sea salt

Boil the potatoes in plenty of salted water until they are very soft when poked with a sharp knife. Drain the spuds and mash them. I use a mouli, which makes a lovely lump-free mash. Stir through the milk and butter. You may need a bit more or less milk but you want to end up with a fairly soft mash. Add the salt (you may need more than you think).

Sometimes if I am feeling poncy, I use an electric whisk to whisk the spuds – it makes them extra smooth and light. My son Felix likes a grating of nutmeg in his mash. It is very good.

TIP Try adding a few parsnips or sweet potatoes to mash for a great alternative. Use 800g/1lb 12oz Maris Piper potatoes and 500g/1lb 2oz parsnips or sweet potatoes (peeled and cubed). Boil and mash as above.

ROSTI — TO SERVE TWO TO FOUR

2 large floury potatoes *peeled and grated*
1 tsp finely chopped fresh rosemary

3 tbsp olive oil
sea salt and freshly ground black pepper

Rinse the grated potato with plenty of cold water, then dry thoroughly in a tea towel. Mix the rosemary into the potatoes and season.

Heat the oil on a medium heat in a large non-stick pan. Divide the potato into four balls and place in the pan. Fry for a couple of minutes, then flatten with a fish slice or spatula. Keep squashing the potato cakes throughout the cooking. Fry until the bottom of the potato cake is crisp and brown – this should take around 15 minutes. Carefully turn the cake over and cook for another 15 minutes.

POMMES DAUPHINOISES — TO SERVE SIX

5 large baking potatoes
150ml/5fl oz milk
150ml/5fl oz double cream
3 cloves of garlic *peeled and finely chopped*

1 tablespoon freshly grated Parmesan
100g/3½oz butter
sea salt and freshly ground black pepper

Preheat the oven to 160°C/325°F/gas mark 3. Peel the potatoes and slice into thin discs, either with a food processor or with a mandolin. (You can do it by hand but it does take ages.) Wash the discs of potato in cold water, to remove excess starch, and pat dry with a tea towel, keeping a few of the best discs to finish the top. Place the potatoes in a baking dish with the milk, cream and garlic, season and mix well with your hands. Push the potatoes flat into the dish then arrange the remaining potato discs in a neat pattern on the top. Sprinkle on the Parmesan, dot the top with butter and season.

Bake in the oven for 1 hour until golden on top. To test if it is cooked, prod with a knife – it should feel soft.

ROSEMARY ROAST NEW POTATOES — TO SERVE SIX

8 cloves of garlic *in their skins*
1kg/2¼lb clean new potatoes *cut into quarters*
8 x 5cm/2 inch sprigs of rosemary

1½ tbsp olive oil
sea salt and freshly ground black pepper

Totally easy and super yummy. No messing about with peeling or boiling. Preheat the oven to 220°C/425°F/gas mark 7. Put all the ingredients in an ovenproof dish (it needs to be big enough for them to lie in one layer). Mix well with your hands until the spuds are all coated in oil, then pop in the oven for about 50 minutes. After 25 minutes give them a good stir so they brown all over, then roast for a further 25 minutes or until crisp and golden.

A

artichoke and lemon soup 19
Asian spices, pork with 72
aubergines: aubergine and lamb soup 50
　aubergine stew 169
　caponata 174
　imam bayildi with dill rice 178
　melanzane alla parmigiana 176
　ratatouille 177

B

barley: beef and barley soup 12
　Scotch broth 48
beans 186
　black bean and pork belly soup 65
　black bean and red pepper stew 172
　Boston baked beans 74
　Caribbean coconut curry 117
　cassoulet 78
　chicken, chorizo and butterbean stew 116
　chorizo and butter bean stew 173
　Crazy Homies exterminator chilli 36
　lamb with preserved lemon 60
　Mexican chicken soup 106
　Mexican lamb 57
　pancetta and white bean soup 64
　ribollita 88
　soup au pistou 157
　spiced lamb with beans 53
　white bean and butternut squash soup 153
beef 10–43
　beef and barley soup 12
　beef, beer and mushroom stew 26
　boeuf bourguignonne 29
　boeuf en daube 30
　brown Windsor soup 17
　Burgundy beef with wild mushrooms 18
　carbonnade à la flamande 38
　Crazy Homies exterminator chilli 36
　hearty beef soup 14
　Jeremy Lee's featherblade 32–3
　Mr Pianim's beef curry 24
　oxtail soup 15
　shabu-shabu 21
　stock 184
beer: beef, beer and mushroom stew 26
　carbonnade à la flamande 38
　hunter's stew 76
beetroot: borscht 161
bisque, Terence Conran's 129
black beans: black bean and pork soup 65
　black bean and red pepper stew 172
black pudding: Creole gumbo 145
boeuf bourguignonne 29
boeuf en daube 30
bollito misto 35
borlotti beans: soup au pistou 157
　spiced lamb with beans 53
borscht 161
Boston baked beans with pork belly 74
bouillabaisse with rouille 137–8
bread: corn bread 134
　garlic croutons 137–8
　seeded rolls 152
Broadbent, Mark 168
brown Windsor soup 17
Burgundy beef with wild mushrooms 18
burrida, langoustine and clam 127
butter beans: chicken, chorizo and butterbean stew 116
　chorizo and butter bean stew 173

C

cabbage: cabbage and pork pot 71
　hunter's stew 76　pheasant with red cabbage 94
caldo de pollo 106
caponata 174
carbonnade à la flamande 38
Caribbean coconut curry 117
cassoulet 78
cawl, Welsh 46
cheese: aubergine stew with halloumi 169
　squash and goat's cheese stew 170
　cheesy dumplings 26
　melanzane alla parmigiana 176
　onion soup 162
chestnuts, daube of venison and 93
chicken 100–21
　bollito misto 35
　Caribbean coconut curry 117
　chicken and mushroom stew 113
　chicken, chorizo and butterbean stew 116
　chicken curry for little chickens 120
　coq au vin 111–12
　cream of chicken soup with tarragon 104
　Creole prawn and chicken gumbo 145
　fragrant chicken stew 114
　hot and sour chicken and exotic mushroom soup 110
　jambalaya 143
　lemon chicken with spinach 118
　Mexican chicken soup 106
　Mum's chicken soup 107
　my soothing chicken and noodle soup 102
　sloppy, spicy, red chicken stew 121
　soothing matzo ball soup 108
　stock 185
chickpeas: aubergine, lamb and chickpea soup 50
　lemon chicken with spinach 118
chillies: black bean and pork belly soup 65
　Caribbean coconut curry 117
　corn bread 134
　Crazy Homies exterminator chilli 36
　gambas pil-pil 140
　red duck curry 97–8
chorizo: chicken and butterbean stew 116
　chorizo and butter bean stew 173
　jambalaya 143
chowder, corn 133
clams: langoustine and clam burrida 127
coconut milk: Caribbean coconut curry 117
　Goan prawn curry 139
　red duck curry 97–8
cod: bouillabaisse with rouille 137–8
　corn chowder 133
Conran, Caroline 113
Conran, Terence 129
Conran, Tom 36
Conran, Vicki 59
consommé, pheasant with baby veg 82
coq au vin 111–12
corn bread 134
corn chowder 133
Corrigan, Richard 84–5
courgettes: ratatouille 177
crab: Terence Conran's bisque 129
Crazy Homies exterminator chilli 36
Creole prawn and chicken gumbo 145
croutons, garlic 137–8
cucumber: gazpacho 165

D

daubes: boeuf en daube 30
　daube of venison 93
duck: cassoulet 78
　red duck curry 97–8

F

featherblade, Jeremy Lee's 32–3
fish 122–47
　stock 185
foie gras: green pea, foie gras and pancetta cappuccino 68–9
fragrant chicken stew 114

G

Galvin, Chris 93
gambas pil-pil 140
game 80–99
garlic: garlic croutons 137–8
　rosemary roast new potatoes 188
gazpacho 165
Goan prawn curry 139
goat's cheese: butternut squash and goat's cheese stew 170
gumbo, Creole prawn and chicken 145
Gyngell, Skye 124

H

'The Hairy Bikers' 52
hake: bouillabaisse with rouille 137–8
　langoustine and clam burrida 127
halibut: bouillabaisse with rouille 137–8
ham: bollito misto 35
hare: split lentil soup with braised hare 84–5
haricot beans: Boston baked beans with pork belly
　cassoulet 78
　lamb with preserved lemon 60
　pancetta and white bean soup 64
　soup au pistou 157
hearty beef soup 14
Highland games 87
Hix, Mark 132
hotpot, Lancashire 52
Huang, Ching-he 110
hunter's stew 76

I

imam bayildi with dill rice 178
inky squid stew 144
Irish rabbit stew 92
Irish stew 59

J

jambalaya 143

K

kidney beans: Crazy Homies exterminator chilli

L

lamb 44–61
　aubergine, lamb and chickpea soup 50
　Irish stew 59
　lamb and noodles 49
　lamb shanks with caramelised onion 54
　lamb with preserved lemon 60
　Lancashire hotpot 52
　Mexican lamb 57
　Scotch broth 48
　Spanish lamb shoulder with tomatoes 58
　spiced lamb with beans 53
　stock 184

Welsh cawl 46
Lancashire hotpot 52
langoustines: bouillabaisse 137–8
  langoustine and clam burrida 127
  spicy Thai broth 130
Lee, Jeremy 32–3
leeks: leek and potato soup 150
  vichyssoise with oysters 132
lemon: artichoke and lemon soup 19
  lamb with preserved lemon 60
  lemon chicken with spinach 118
  Mum's chicken soup 107
lentils: hearty beef soup 14
  Jeremy Lee's featherblade 32–3
  lentils with Italian sausage 73
  split lentil soup with braised hare 84–5
lobster: lobster bonne femme 124
  Terence Conran's bisque 129

M

mashed potatoes 187
matzo ball soup 108
melanzane alla parmigiana 176
Mexican chicken soup 106
Mexican lamb 57
Mr Pianim's beef curry 24
moules marinières 146
Mum's chicken soup 107
mushrooms: beef and mushroom stew 26
  boeuf bourguignonne 29
  Burgundy beef with wild mushrooms 18
  chicken and mushroom stew 113
  coq au vin 111–12
  hot and sour chicken soup 110
  hunter's stew 76
  pheasant and sausage stew 99
  shabu-shabu 21
mussels: bouillabaisse with rouille 137–8
  moules marinières 146

N

nettle soup 168
noodles: lamb and noodles 49
  my soothing chicken and noodle soup 102
  shabu-shabu 21
Novelli, Jean-Christophe 68–9

O

onions: carbonnade à la flamande 38
  coq au vin 111–12
  hunter's stew 76
  lamb shanks with caramelised onion 54
  onion soup 162
  osso bucco and risotto Milanese 41–2
oxtail soup 15
oysters: oyster and watercress soup 125
  vichyssoise with oysters 132

P

pancetta: cassoulet 78
  green pea and foie gras cappuccino 68–9
  pancetta and white bean soup 64
pasta: fresh pasta 103
  pasta in brodo 23
peppers: black bean and pepper stew 172
  gazpacho 165
  hearty beef soup 14
  jambalaya 143
  ratatouille 177
  sloppy, spicy, red chicken stew 121
pheasant: Highland games 87
  pheasant and sausage stew 99

pheasant consommé with baby veg 82
  pheasant with red cabbage 94
pigeon: ribollita 88
pinto beans: Mexican lamb 57
  ribollita 88
pistou, soup au 157
polenta: corn bread 134
pommes dauphinoises 188
pork 62–79
  black bean and pork belly soup 65
  Boston baked beans with pork belly 74
  cabbage and pork pot 71
  hunter's stew 76
  pork and prune stew 79
  pork with Asian spices 72
port: daube of venison 93
  venison with port and plums 91
potatoes: Irish stew 59
  Lancashire hotpot 52
  leek and potato soup 150
  lobster bonne femme 124
  mashed potatoes 187
  pommes dauphinoises 188
  rosemary roast new potatoes 188
  rösti 187
  vichyssoise with oysters 132
prawns: Creole gumbo 145
  gambas pil-pil 140
  Goan prawn curry 139
  jambalaya 143
  spicy Thai broth with prawns 130
pulses 186

Q

quinces, daube of venison 93

R

rabbit stew, Irish 92
ratatouille 177
red duck curry 97–8
red kidney beans: Caribbean curry 117
ribollita 88
rolls, seeded 152
root soup 158
rosemary roast new potatoes 188
rösti 187

S

sausages: butternut squash and soup 66
  cassoulet 78
  chicken, chorizo and butterbean stew 116
  chorizo and butter bean stew 173
  hunter's stew 76
lentils with Italian sausage 73
  pheasant and sausage stew 99
Scotch broth 48
seeded rolls 152
shabu-shabu 21
Spanish lamb shoulder with olives 58
spiced lamb with beans 53
spicy Thai broth with prawns 130
spinach, lemon chicken with 118
squash: butternut squash stew 170
  butternut squash and sausage soup 66
  fragrant chicken stew 114
  white bean and squash soup 153
squid: inky squid stew 144
  langoustine and clam burrida 127
sweet potatoes: Caribbean curry 117
  root soup 158
sweetcorn: black bean and pork soup 65
  black bean and red pepper stew 172
    corn bread and chowder 133/134

T

tagliatelle 103
tarragon, cream of chicken soup with 104
tofu: shabu-shabu 21
tomatoes: aubergine stew 169
  black bean and pork belly soup 65
  boeuf en daube 30
  bouillabaisse with rouille 137–8
  chicken chorizo stew 116
  chicken curry for little chickens 120
  Crazy Homies exterminator chilli 36
  cream of tomato soup 165
  Creole prawn and chicken gumbo 145
  gazpacho 165
  hearty beef soup 14
  inky squid stew 144
  lamb with preserved lemon 60
  melanzane alla parmigiana 176
  Mexican lamb 57
  osso bucco and risotto Milanese 41–2
  ratatouille 177
  sloppy, spicy, red chicken stew 121
  Spanish lamb shoulder with tomatoes 58
  spiced lamb with beans 53

V

veal: bollito misto 35
  brown Windsor soup 17
  osso bucco and risotto Milanese 41–2
vegetables 148–79
  artichoke and lemon soup 19
  bouillabaisse with rouille 137–8
  butternut squash and sausage soup 66
  cabbage and pork pot 71
  Highland games 87
  Irish rabbit stew 92
   oxtail soup 15
  pheasant consommé with baby veg 82
  ribollita 88
  root soup 158
  Scotch broth 48
  soup au pistou 157
  venison and root vegetables 90
  Welsh cawl 46
vegetarian soups: borscht 161
  cream of tomato soup 165
  gazpacho 165
  leek and potato soup 150
  nettle soup 168
  root soup 158
  soup au pistou 157
  white bean and squash soup 153
vegetarian stews: aubergine stew 169
  black bean and red pepper stew 172
  butternut squash stew 170
  caponata 174
  imam bayildi with dill rice 178
  melanzane alla parmigiana 176
  ratatouille 177
venison: daube of venison 93
  Highland games 87
  venison and root vegetables 90
  venison with port and plums 91
vichyssoise with oysters 132

W

watercress: oyster and watercress soup 125
  watercress soup 154
Welsh cawl 46
white bean soup 153
Worrall Thompson, Antony 153

Thank You

Of course this book was not written by me alone and in fact the bulk of the work was done by an incredible army of angels. I would like to thank them all for being so incredibly fantastic and making the writing and production of the book such a joy.

Harriet Arbuthnot for being my bright and brilliant right hand.

Helena for being wonderful and keeping my world in order.

Felix and Coco my inspiration and for all the giggling.

Lizzy Gray for all-round fabulousness, patience and thoughtfulness.

David Loftus for the stunning pictures, a joyous shoot and friendship.

Jenny Heller for believing in me, your courage and vision.

Cheryl for all your generosity and guidance.

Charlotte and **Jenny** for making me look so fabulous.

Grechen, **Vivian** and **Euan** at the Laquer Chest for the gorgeous props and most welcome cup of tea in town.

Julian, **Jodie** and **Carol** at Portmeirion for being wonderful and magnificent to work with.

Rosie and **Fania** for giving your best.

Susanna Cook for a beautiful book.

Sarah Canet for your constant brilliance.

All my magnificent family and friends for your love.

Humungous thanks to everyone for the sensational guest recipes that have been contributed.

First published in 2008 by Collins, an imprint of HarperCollins Publishers
77-85 Fulham Palace Road London W6 8JB

www.collins.co.uk
Collins is a registered trademark of HarperCollins Publishers

Text © Sophie Conran, 2008
Photography © David Loftus, 2008

The author retains the moral rights to be identified as the author of this work. All rights reserved. No parts of this publication may be reproduced, stored in a retrieval system or transmitted in any form or by any means, electronic, mechanical, photocopying, recording or otherwise, without the prior permission of the publishers.

A catalogue record for this book is available from the British Library.

ISBN 978-0-00-727991-3
Editorial Director: Jenny Heller
Senior Development Editor: Lizzy Gray
Editor: Lesley Robb
Design: **allies**design.com Susanna Cook & Amy Joyce
Cover Design: Anna Martin

Colour reproduction by Colourscan, Singapore
Printed and bound by Rotolito Lombarda, Italy

Mixed Sources
Product group from well-managed forests and other controlled sources
www.fsc.org Cert no. SW-COC-1806
© 1996 Forest Stewardship Council

FSC